365 Ways to Raise Funds
for Your Nonprofit

Dear KRIS,

I hope your generous spirit becomes Pandemic!

Happy fund Raising!

Cheers,

April

D1452155

Dear Kris,

I hope your generous
spirit becomes a Pandemic!
Keep that viral Buzzing!

Cheers,

[signature]

365 WAYS TO RAISE FUNDS FOR YOUR NONPROFIT

Practical Ideas for Every Not-for-Profit Organization

APRIL R. JERVIS, MBA

Universal-Publishers
Boca Raton

365 Ways to Raise Funds for Your Nonprofit:
Practical Ideas for Every Not-for-Profit Organization

Universal-Publishers
Boca Raton, Florida • USA
2011

ISBN-10: 1-61233-030-4
ISBN-13: 978-1-61233-030-3

www.universal-publishers.com

Cover photo @Cutcaster.com/Cienpies Design

Author cover photo by Ben Van Sickle

Cover design by Shereen Siddiqui

Library of Congress Cataloging-in-Publication Data

Jervis, April R., 1981-
  365 ways to raise funds for your nonprofit : practical ideas for every
not-for-profit organization / April R. Jervis.
     p. cm.
  ISBN-13: 978-1-61233-030-3 (pbk. : alk. paper)
  ISBN-10: 1-61233-030-4 (pbk. : alk. paper)
  1. Fund raising. 2. Nonprofit organizations. I. Title.
  HV41.2.J47 2011
  658.15'224--dc23

                                                2011028257

ACKNOWLEDGMENTS

I am thankful to my husband, Marc Mar-Yohana, a real renaissance man, for his sense of humor and friendship. Marc, I hope our children get your intelligence and my punctuality. I would like to thank my daughter Constance for filling my life with joy and love. Constance, without you, I would not need to write a book to save for your college fund.

I would like to thank my mother, Cindy Wolavka, for spending hours helping me to learn to read, amongst countless other things. Thank you to my stepfather, Robert Wolavka, for encouraging my graduate school education and for patiently listening during the innumerable calls when I complained about it.

I would like to thank my father, Richard Jervis, for helping make my charitable endeavors international in scope and for loaning me his car for years at time despite my driving record. Thank you to my stepmother, Juliet Jervis, for teaching me that adding water is not really cooking.

Special thanks to my grandma, Harriet Vollmer. Her beliefs in God, hard work, and boundless generosity have guided my life. A debt of gratitude is owed to my late grandfather, William Vollmer, who never mentioned that when I was a child he rescued me from a boating accident.

Thanks to my siblings Nicholas Jervis, William Jervis, and Robin Wolavka. Only Nicholas could make a reading of a car's owner manual a laugh out loud theatrical event. Without William's fearlessness we wouldn't have spent an incredibly exhilarating afternoon in an abandoned London carnival. Thanks to Robin for the two-person dance parties and for letting me play with your hair.

I could fill volumes with thanks to friends, so I will limit myself to the help I received with this book. I want to express my gratitude to my friend Carla Kilgore, who helped edit this book. I want to be Carla when I grow up.

I am grateful to those who reviewed this book. They are listed at www.apriljervis.com. Thanks to Jeff Young at Universal Publishers for his help cultivating and publishing this text. I would like to thank you, the reader, for buying a copy of this book and for participating in the world of fundraising. Our communities would be lost without the nonprofit industry's professionals, volunteers, donors, and institutions. You make everything from research to hot lunches possible. Thank you.

ABOUT THE AUTHOR

April R. Jervis is a nonprofit professional with over ten years of experience. She has served as a volunteer, coordinator, trainer, executive director, spokesperson, founder, administrator, and board member for a cornucopia of organizations. April earned a Bachelor of Science from Indiana State University and a Masters of Business Administration from Loyola University of Chicago. She also received a Certificate in Nonprofit Management from the United Nation's Mandated Universidad para la Paz (University of Peace). April credits much of her success to the leaders in the nonprofit, social entrepreneurship, and governmental sectors who have mentored and guided her through her career.

April has helped a wide variety of nonprofit organizations improve their operations, manage their resources, create and execute strategic plans, and of course, fundraise. Her causes have ranged from refugee service providers to organizations providing direct care to the disabled.

April is a firm believer in volunteerism. She has donated her time to numerous organizations, beginning with the American Red Cross at age 14. She hopes to live a long life of assistance, and has gratitude to those whose service has made her professional accomplishments possible.

April currently lives with her family in the central United States. She enjoys international travel, following current events, playing games, and trying new restaurants with her husband Marc. She relaxes by cultivating her vegetable garden, watching movies, reading, and listening to podcasts. She cherishes celebrating special occasions with family and friends. She is an avid crafter. April loves reading and playing with her daughter Constance. April and Marc get great pleasure from watching as Constance learns and grows.

TABLE OF CONTENTS

FOREWORD

Whereas in times of economic abundance, fundraising efforts can rely on the generosity of those with more privileges, times of economic scarcity bring forth another process: fundraising as a community-building event. The tradition of communities coming together to support causes that they believe in is a principle that America is built on. A fundraiser can make one's cause a community experience that brings people together not only to create a better future, but also to foster a more cohesive presence. The process of energizing a community for fundraising is itself a community-building experience that goes beyond simply donating money for a particular cause: the community is strengthened through the collaborative experience of fundraising.

April Jervis' book is based on this paradigm, and provides hundreds of practical examples for application by a diversity of groups to activate and initiate community-building experiences. As a side effect, these events create the funds needed to expand the projects further. The best fundraising efforts result in a mutual experience in which both the giver and the receiver feel equally enriched. We recommend April's book as a pathway towards this destination.

The Deep Democracy Institute is a leadership and consulting non-profit organization with US headquarters and sister organizations in the Ukraine, Russia, Kenya, Netherlands, and the Palestinian territories. We are faced everyday with funding issues, not only those of our own organization, but also of the many organizations that we assist in grant writing. Of the many books that we have encountered on this topic, April Jervis' *365 Ways...* is the most practical and creative text. Its strength lies especially in its solutions for a wide diversity of organizations. Every non-profit is different, and therefore has different funding needs. Jervis has solutions for all of them.

DR. MAX SCHUPBACH & DR. ELLEN SCHUPBACH

The Deep Democracy Institute

FUNDRAISING
METHODS

1. POT LUCK TO GIVE A BUCK

A pot luck, or pitch-in, as it called in some regions, is an event where each attendee brings a dish and everyone eats together in a buffet format. This makes for an easy, low-overhead fundraiser. Common in religious organizations for years, this type of event can be expanded to nearly any organization. It works best in groups that have a membership base: organizers can ask each member to bring a dish and to contribute. Attendees can be encouraged to donate what they would spend for a lunch out. This creates an atmosphere where individuals can donate as they are able.

For example, I organized a pot luck event for a financial literacy organization that we titled, "Pot Luck to Give a Buck." The title made it clear to attendees that they were being asked to bring food and a few dollars to kick in to the organization, too. As the organizer, I contacted local grocery stores and found one that was willing to donate a $25 gift card to the event. This covered the costs of dishes, silverware, beverages, paper table clothes, and chips. Holding the event in the office served the dual purpose of keeping down costs and exposing members to the organization's location and marketing materials. Attendees used the event as an opportunity to network.

When approaching a grocery store for a donation, keep in mind that most stores:

• Require requests in writing at least a month before the event. Call the location to get the store manager's name. Envelopes addressed to a person are much more likely to get a personal response.

• Give a maximum of $25 in store credit at the store level. For larger donations, you must go through the corporate headquarters giving program. Information about this program is available on corporate websites, typically under the heading "community."

• Require you to come into the store to collect the gift card. Don't bother asking for support from a store that is so far away that you'll burn more than $25 in gas getting there to pick up the card. To save time, purchase the items you need while collecting the card.

• Must have a copy of the tax exempt certificate and federal tax identification number to give you the donation. It is easiest to send a copy of these items with the donation request letter.

• Often wait until the last minute to notify the applicant that they have been granted the donation. If they are not awarding the gift, they may not call at all. To prevent a last minute drive across town, call to follow up on your donation request two weeks before the event.

This event is informal and social in nature, so keep the invitations the same way. I have used personal emails, but you could also use a free online service like Evite.com. The benefit to using Evite over personal email is that they track RSVPs for you. Email, however, provides the benefit of personal contact to help encourage attendance.

Another element to be aware of is that attendees frequently bring dessert items because they are cheap and easy to prepare or purchase. As a result, you may need to supplement the menu by preparing a main dish or having a local restaurant donate one. Prepare labels in advance that show a dish's contents, for instance, "Spaghetti, vegan, and gluten free." Post-its can be colorful and easy, but card stock cards can be used for a more formal occasion. If you need to print labels in advance, ask attendees to RSVP with the type of dish they're bringing. Keep in mind that the more you ask people to bring, the less they're likely to donate in cash at the event. Make it easy to donate with donation tins and a mention of their location. Be sure to mention the importance of the cause in your welcoming speech.

2. LETTER-WRITING CAMPAIGN

Letter-writing campaigns are an old standby of fundraising. They have been around since organized mail delivery and still exist today because they are effective. One major development is their increased cost. The cost of stamps, envelopes, ink, paper, and staff time continues to increase. To make this venture a good investment, you should only send letters to individuals with a demonstrated interest in your organization or cause. A great rule of thumb is: if someone has donated before, they are likely to do so again. Just don't ask too frequently or they'll take their money somewhere they feel it is more appreciated.

Some corporations sell lead lists to charities with the names and addresses of individuals they believe are likely donors. I have worked with organizations where this has been helpful and others where it has not. I recommend not taking the gamble if your resources are limited.

There are a couple of simple ways to construct your own mailing lists. Begin your list with past donors. I recommend using a simple data management tool to input the names and addresses that can easily be used in a mail merge. Then add recent event attendees and past supporters. Finally, look for individuals in the community who are in fields that make it probable that they will see the value of your work. For instance, if you are raising money for a blood bank, consider sending solicitations to healthcare professionals in the area. Many corporations list their key employees' names and titles on their websites.

Keep in mind the following additional tips when constructing a letter of solicitation:

• Begin with a call to action. Catch the recipient's attention and explain why they should act now. You will need to show the value of your cause and persuade the donor to act immediately. Statistics often work well.

• Make it personal. Address it to the person and don't misspell their name.

• Include sincere thanks for previous support. Discuss what the organization has done that has made a difference in the local community of the recipient.

• If you are hoping for a large amount of money, consider a hand written note and business card, too.

• Do everything you can to avoid looking like a mass mailing. If you can hand-sign each letter and/or hand-address each envelope (with the help of volunteers), then do so.

• Make it easy to give by including a donation slip (easily put on the bottom of the letter page) and a return envelope that is pread-dressed to you. Include on the donation slip space for credit or debit card information, expiration date, code, signature, and billing zip code. Additionally, include spaces for the donor to check if they have enclosed a check or need to update their address.

3. AMAZON ASSOCIATES

Many corporations have profit sharing programs. Amazon.com's is unique because it is easy to set up online and completely website-based. This partnership provides additional benefits because of the enormous market share of Amazon.com in the retail space. Your supporters are going to shop Amazon.com with or without your participation in the Amazon Associate program; why not get a portion of the sales?

Set up is easy. You'll need your federal tax identification number, physical mailing address, and an Amazon.com account. Go to Amazon.com's site and click on "Amazon Associates." There you can set up an account. The site will take you step-by-step through the process of setting up a widget for your organization's site and/or social networking page. It will provide you the widget code in HTML. You'll simply have to copy it and paste it into your page. If you use an IT company, it's easy for them to insert the code for you if you email it to them. The widget can be anything from a simple link to a large banner advertisement. I prefer the search box because it is unlikely to offend any supporter who comes to your site, and is always in season so it won't have to be updated regularly.

As your supporters visit your site, they will see the Amazon widget advertisement. If they click on it and purchase any item through that link, your organization will receive a portion of the proceeds from the sale. The portion that your organization receives is determined in advance by Amazon and depends on your site's traffic and audience.

Some special tips to keep in mind while setting up your Amazon Associates account include:

• Amazon provides extra rewards for requesting checks less frequently and for transferring funds electronically. If you can wait to receive checks, then it is advantageous to do so.

• Amazon only provides the code for HTML. If you need XML or another type of code, try various free online conversion services to get the code to work. Amazon will not provide any technical support to Associates who need help getting their widgets to work in their sites.

• Use Amazon's link checker to ensure that the widget on your site works before your supporters try to use it. This will ensure that you will receive credit for those purchases.

• When setting up your account, make sure to enter every version of the site address so Amazon knows what traffic is yours.

• You can put more than one widget on your site or widgets on more than one page. Using more than one will increase purchases.

When I set up an Amazon Associates account for a foundation, I made a special webpage for it. Then, I promoted that page through e-newsletters, on other pages of the site, and on our social networking pages. I asked our supporters to bookmark the page and go through it when making their holiday purchases. As a result, Amazon sent us checks for 4% of all sales. The percentage the organization receives from Amazon varies based on the kind and amount of traffic to your site, as well as the products purchased.

4. DIAL FOR DOLLARS

Recent legislation and public sentiment are against cold calling as a form of fundraising. If you are going to "dial for dollars," call only individuals who have a previous relationship with the organization. Don't call during the work day, dinner time, or late in the evening. This leaves small pockets of time that must be adjusted for time zones.

Have staff and volunteers practice their pitches before they dial anyone. Keep statistics and water close by the phones. Also, keep credit card donation slips and lots of pens handy. You can process the donations after the calls have all been made. Use a voiceover IP service, such as Skype, to make calling cheap and convenient from any computer.

Read the name of the person you're calling before dialing, and be sure to determine correct pronunciation. If anyone in the organization (staff or volunteer) knows the potential donor personally or has spoken to them before, have this person make the call. Begin with a personal and friendly introduction and conclude with a thank you, even if the person does not donate. In my experience, mentioning recent progress on the cause and thanking donors for past support goes a long way to ensure that their donations continue. No matter what, do not hang up on the person or become angry.

5. Silent Auction

A silent auction is an auction where attendees bid on items by writing their names and numbers on a bid sheet. This event is a great supplement to a party or other gathering. Display items you are auctioning behind bid sheets, and make sure there is at least one pen per sheet. Announce to everyone the end time for the auction; this is when the last bid will be accepted and the sheets will be collected. Make sure attendees know what forms of payment are accepted and when and how they will collect their winnings. It is simplest and saves on shipping to provide winners with the goods at the event of the event and to collect their check or credit/debit card information after the auction is completed.

A bid sheet should be one sheet of paper. If you feel there will be a lot of bids, go with the legal-sized sheet. In the past, I have been able to get carbon copy paper that transfers bid information onto a second record sheet from FedEx. Attach each sheet to a clip board if table space is limited. Each bid sheet should contain the following information:

• Name of good and corresponding number placed on good for identification

• Description of good

• Donor of item

• Starting price of auction and retail price of item

• Increments in which bidding can occur. I recommend making this the same for each item to prevent confusion.

• Lines going down sheet for bidders to insert their name, number, and bid

• Space at the bottom of the sheet to record payment information, including the credit/debit card information of the winner, their address, phone, email, and a box to check if they paid in cash or check at the event.

I have organized silent auctions for many different types of nonprofit organizations in many different events, and the secret to success is to not to pay for anything you are auctioning off. All of the auctioned items should be donated by area businesses. You will be surprised and delighted at how eager they are to contribute. Because the auction will have no overhead cost, bids are all profit. Incidentally, I have observed that wine always gets bids.

Attendees may ask you if their purchases are tax deductible. Currently, they can only deduct the amount they spend on the item past its retail value. Their accountant or other tax professional can provide more detailed information.

6. ONLINE AUCTION

An online auction can be a great fundraising tool for organizations with a large sprawling network of supporters. Collect donated items and upload photos of them and logos from their donors onto the site. Write compelling and interesting descriptions. Set a starting bid price well under the actual retail price. Clearly explain any costs and logistics associated with collection of the goods to all bidders. Have a well-advertised start and stop time to the auction. Then let the bidding begin!

Some companies, like 32auctions.com, specialize in online auctions for nonprofit organizations. They allow nonprofits to set different bid increments, buy-it-now prices, and reserve price amounts for each item. These cheap and easy online tools allow even the novice auctioneer to sell goods for their cause. I have used this service for online auctions, and also as a way to build up bids before moving to have the auction conclude in person. It was a great way to expand the audience of a silent auction to all stakeholders.

Some special tips for online auctions are:

• Set all starting prices under 50% of the retail price. This encourages bidding and counter bidding. It also increases the likelihood of impulse and luxury buys.

• Clearly express any limitations on the item. For instance, if the item is 8 hours of handyman services, there may be limitations on how far the individual will travel, on the type of work done, or who pays for materials and equipment.

• Thank the donors with a hyperlink to their websites. Some individuals will choose to purchase services they don't win. This is a great way of thanking your donors for their generous support.

• Clearly and repeatedly explain how payment and distribution of items will occur.

• Find out if the service you are using sends any automated messages to bidders or winners, verify that they are consistent with your auction plans, and ensure they send the goods to the winners.

7. Live Auction

Live auctions are the type of auctions that occur at estate sales or auction houses. An auctioneer sells items during live action bidding. This type of auction can work in conjunction with another event or a simultaneous silent auction.

The success of a live auction is dependent on the charisma of the auctioneer and the interest in the goods being sold. Pick your auctioneer carefully. Extroverts are welcome! If necessary, contact a local auction service about donating their time to your event.

Make sure that all attendees know in advance that there will be a live auction. Make sure that everyone is seated, music has stopped, and all eyes are on the auctioneer before the auction begins. For this reason, live auctions are typically successful after formal dinners. Before the first item has been auctioned, the methods of payment accepted (such as check, credit/debit card, or cash) should be reviewed. The winning bidders should go to a winners table to give their names and numbers after they win a good. Items should not be paid for until after the auction is complete. This encourages bidders to win more than one item and saves time by having them only complete one credit card slip.

When choosing items to be auctioned, it is important to consider your audience. If the event is a golf outing, then bags, clubs or weekends at golf resorts make sense as auction items. If your event is a wine tasting at a winery, consider auction weekends in Napa, a large wine collection, or a wine cellar.

Do not start your auction with your most valuable item. Build to it. On occasion, a shy audience might need a couple of items to get to active bidding and counter bidding. I recommend that planners consider including a bar, even a cash bar, for almost any gathering, dinner or otherwise. Simply holding a glass of wine may make an attendee feel more comfortable raising a hand to bid, even before he or she drinks it.

Purchasing items for an auction is always a gamble. If you cannot get enough appropriate items donated, then speak to vendors about providing items at cost to the organization if someone bids on them. For instance, ask a balloon ride company to offer a ride for two. Then, start the bidding slightly above the price to the organization if the item is purchased. If the item is not won in auction, the organization is not on the hook to pay for it.

8. BOARD MEMBERS

Nonprofit organizations are legally required to have at least three Board Members or a three-person Board of Governors. Most nonprofits have bylaws that require them to have at least five. These individuals provide guidance in the long term goal setting and strategy of the organization. Board Members are typically stakeholders who have a special interest in the cause. They can be founders, former directors or other employees, former clients, funders, etc.

Board Members are a great source for donations. You know that they support the cause and the organization. Many organizations require Board Members to support the charity through fiscal contributions. In my experience, this is typically $1,000 annually; however, it varies based on the size of the organization and the prestige of board membership.

If your charity has this policy and it is not followed, or does not have this policy currently, I recommend that the Executive Director speak to each board member about it personally outside of a board meeting before bringing it up in a board meeting or in another group setting. Additionally, it is helpful in procuring board contributions if you consistently:

• Allow the board to guide how resources are allocated, including who is hired to manage day-to-day expenses

• Make sure the board knows why the donations are needed

• Have a forum for public recognition of board members and other supporters

9. Board Members' Contacts

Board Members are a great source of leads for donations. Their community involvement generally spreads past their board position in your nonprofit. Additionally, if they were personally affected by the cause, then they likely know other community members, family, and friends who are, too.

Suggesting that a board or organization adopt a policy that each board member either gets or gives $1,000 to your organization is a much easier sell then just asking for the direct donation from each board member. This tactic encourages members who do not have large expendable incomes to fundraise for the organization. Speaking personally, I found that my work as a nonprofit professional was appreciated all the more when board members discovered for themselves what hard work it is to raise funds.

These connections also serve as a great way to meet potential new board members. If a board member cares deeply for a cause because they were personally affected by it, and they ask their friends and family to donate, those individuals are now in a dialog about your organization. To make it easier for board members or other volunteers to solicit funds, provide them with brochures or leaflets about the organization, as well as some general information regarding how the donation will be used.

10. EMAIL SOLICITATIONS

Email solicitations pose a challenge to a nonprofit. While they represent a very inexpensive way to encourage donations, sending too many emails will mean that your stakeholders may stop opening them. They may even become irritated with the volume or impersonal nature of your requests and simply mark the organization's emails as spam. However, due to the extremely inexpensive nature of email solicitations, a nonprofit must consider when and how to use them as a tool.

An organization is legally only allowed to send mass emails (emails to large numbers of email addresses that are not personalized to the recipient) to individuals who have subscribed to a newsletter or updates. Most nonprofits are very short staffed and keep their teams hopping. Newsletter writing is not a welcomed addition to anyone's to-do list. However, there are some great and very inexpensive tools out there that make constructing a newsletter and maintaining a subscriber database fast and easy. I recommend the services of ReachMail.net or ConstantContact.com. Both offer free templates online that are accessed through the Internet Explorer browser. Other browsers do not currently allow for all of their features to work properly. Free downloads of Internet Explorer are available at download.com. Keep in mind that most of these services offer free trials and user training.

A newsletter should first discuss organization activities and events. Then, include a solicitation for donations. Highlight the organization's success. Do not send a newsletter more than once a month or more people will opt out, eventually leaving your writer as the only recipient.

In addition to email newsletters, include a link to the organization's donation webpage in all outgoing emails. This is a simple and easy way for individuals to give, as well as to be reminded that as a charitable organization, you are dependent on the generosity of your community to continue to do your work. This passive email solicitation is an easy way to garner support.

11. GARAGE SALE

Garage Sales or Yard Sales are a popular way for people to raise a little cash and clean out their cupboards in the warm months. They are also an easy and fast way for an organization to receive an infusion of cash. You can organize these sales to occur at the charity's office or in the neighborhood of a board member or director. By getting neighbors to participate, you increase the likelihood of foot traffic. Maybe the neighbors will give their proceeds to your organization, too!

Many municipalities have regulations regarding garage sales. For instance, where I currently live, residents may have one per year, no yard sale signs may be posted in public spaces, homeowners are required to provide parking, and the police department must be notified in writing a week before the event.

Collect and clean sale items in advance. Make sure that each item is clearly labeled with a price. A cheap and easy way to do this is by using a sharpie marker on masking tape. Simply write the price and stick it to the good in a place where it can easily be removed without damaging the item.

If weather allows, choose a yard sale over a garage sale. Yard sales make it easy for those driving through the neighborhood to see what types of items you have for sale from the street before stopping and walking up to the house or office. They also make it easier for individuals who might not have seen your signs to see the sale. Items that sell well are furniture, fixtures, and appliances.

If possible, put the organization's name and logo on your fliers. In the past, I have promoted yard sales through:

- Fliers on cars in the nearby commuter parking lots

- Leaflets in area coffee shops and bookstores

- Leaflets in neighbors' mailboxes

- Listing the best items on Craigslist with photos, with the buyer information instructing interested persons to come to the garage sale to buy

Remember to only sell what you can live without. Don't part with anything of sentimental value or you will regret it later. Consider scheduling the sale on two or three consecutive days, such as Memorial or Labor Day weekend. If your area has a weekend when they promote yard sales, participate in that. You won't believe the difference that group participation will make in garnering attendance. Be willing to make deals as the sale concludes. This is especially important if you have no use for the items remaining.

Remember that many states require nonprofit organizations to give items of value (such as large pieces of furniture or computers) to another tax-exempt charity, as opposed to giving them to a friend or throwing them away at the end of the event.

12. Bake Sale

Bake sales have long been a staple of school and church group fundraising. However, they also work great as a supplement to causal gatherings for any nonprofit organization. A lobbying group for domestic violence shelters recently raised funds by selling apple pies from their downtown Chicago office. Their Executive Director made the pies and all of the staff members worked together to get stakeholders, neighbors, and everyone else in the office to buy one.

Bake sales are a fun and easy way to raise a little cash. Simply provide a wide variety of treats that are all clearly labeled with:

- The price

- Any allergy information (such as: contains nuts)

- Any special dietary considerations (such as: gluten free or vegan)

Remember to check with your local municipality to determine if there are any regulations you must follow when planning your sale. Publicizing the sale to nearby workers, neighbors, etc. in advance will mean that attendees can plan ahead to bring cash or checks. Provide a wide variety of portion sizes and prices. Sell a plate of five cookies, as well as a dozen on a decorative plate. Sell a piece of apple pie, as well as an entire pie. In this way, you are likely to get those hungry now, as well as those planning for their family dinner or an upcoming gathering.

Have lots of volunteers ready to take cash or checks. This will keep the line moving and increase sales. If possible, have volunteers wear aprons to reinforce that the items are homemade. At one sale, we hung a sign that said, "Our secret ingredient is love." It caught the eye of passersby and helped us reel in someone new to the sale.

13. THRIFT STORE

Thrift Stores, or resale shops as they are sometimes called, seem like no-fail business ventures for charities but there are many ways that they can be big losers. Planning can save you time and money.

Treat the opening of your thrift store as if you were an entrepreneur preparing a business plan. Many business schools require Masters of Business Administration students (future MBAs) to work on business plans for entrepreneurs free of charge as part of their studies. Speak to the local business schools about securing their free services.

Calculate staff costs including hourly pay, benefits, payroll taxes, training time, insurance, sick time, maternity/paternity leave, and bereavement days, and tax preparation costs. Try to get donated space for the store in an easily accessible area. If you cannot get space donated, then speak to your local elected official about using vacant or abandoned space. Consider the location of competitors and your customers when securing a location. Other overhead costs include credit card and cash register equipment and fees, electricity, water, bathroom supplies, hangers, shelves, lawn maintenance, licenses, and other taxes.

Offering pickup services for furniture and other large donations is a money pit. Avoid it completely if possible. It is better to not have an old stained sofa than it is to spend more in procuring it than you will get for it. Instead, either avoid selling furniture not brought into the facility or work with local delivery companies to get a certain number of donated pickups each year.

Offer one sale day a week where everything is on sale to get more foot traffic into your store. There is no need to offer a dressing room. Patrons will just have to gamble that the $1 sweater they're buying will fit. This saves you on the space and a staff member to monitor it.

When purchasing store furnishings, contact business liquidation companies to see if they have anything they can either donate to you or provide you with at cost. This way, you don't have to spend a fortune on fixtures such as clothing racks.

When establishing your initial inventory, consider having large collection events at local civic or religious centers. Ongoing collection should happen at the store's location. You can also add to your collection sites through community locations or bins around town. Speak to industrial business vendors about the costs in advance to determine if bins and their collection are worth the financial invest-ment.

Maintain a no-return policy. The items are already used, so it would be impossible for staff to determine if they were used by the individual returning them. Clearly communicate this policy through signs at each cash register.

Hold a grand opening event and promote it like crazy! Opening your first location is a very big deal! Promote it to all the local media and all of your stakeholders. The press will bring in customers and new supporters to the cause. Also, your preparation is finally paying off, so celebrate it!

14. CHILI COOK-OFF

The brilliance of the Chili Cook-Off is its ability to draw a crowd. Hold the event indoors in a well-known and donated space. Electric-ity is a challenge. Many chefs will want to bring hot plates or other heating elements to maintain the warmth of the food. This keeps the chili tasty and safe for consumption. However, it also means you will need a space with many outlets and tables. You may need to provide extra cords and power strips. Speak to the facilities manager in ad-vance about the electrical capacity. To make the event livelier and more social, try to get a band or DJ to donate services for a couple of hours while the competition is being held. Providing cheap activi-ties for kids like chili coloring sheets with boxes of loose crayons will keep children occupied and parents happy.

Have each chef register in advance to participate. Require each to pay a small fee to compete (such as $5) and award half of the Chef's registration fees as the prize to the winner. See if a local gourmet grocery store or kitchen supply store will donate gift cer-tificates or gift baskets for winners. Small plaques and trophies are a must. The trophies should be provided the day of the event and the plaques can be inscribed and delivered later.

Awards should include a Grand Prize and a People's Choice Award. Have three to five local restaurateurs serve as taste testers for the competition's Grand Prize award. Title your grand prize. Make it the kind of title a cook or restaurant would want to brag about, such as "Best Chili in Dallas 2011." Attendees will judge the People's Choice Award. Require that each chef bring enough cups of warm chili and a ladle to the event to allow attendees and judges to taste it. When they arrive, provide each of them a with a paper sign displaying their name, assigned number for voting, and any special information about their chili such as "vegetarian" or "extremely hot." You may want each chef to rate the hotness of their chili on a five pepper scale.

Charge attendees $1 per three little disposable cups to taste any three chilis they would like. They can buy as many disposable cups as they want. Chili is available as supplies last. Give each attendee one ballot to drop in a box. On the ballot, have a list of each chef and their number, such as "7 Momma Rosa's Turkey Chili." Make a limit of one vote per attendee.

To increase the proceeds from the event, the organization should sell cans or bottles of soda, beer, and chips. I participated in one cook-off where a local bakery donated several sheet cakes which were sold by the piece for $1. Provide water for free to everyone. When attendees arrive, have them sign a waiver of liability for your organization and your participating cooks. You do not want your charity brought down by a lawsuit against you and the "Hottest Chili in the South."

Make the award ceremony seem as grand as possible. Drum rolls and applause are welcome! Don't take so long to tabulate votes that the attendees have already left. Ask a local politician to hand out the award. This will increase the likelihood of press coverage. Press is important because it will encourage restaurants to compete. Hold the event annually and make the date predictable: for example, on the second Saturday in October. This will help build attendance and turn your event into a family tradition for many community members.

15. WEBSITE

It continues to shock me how many nonprofit organizations do not have a way to accept contributions via their website. Websites should have information regarding how to mail in donations via check, but that is not enough. A link should be provided on each page, including the home page, which takes viewers directly to the donation page.

A donation page should have a simple and secure form that accepts credit and debit purchases. It should work with any type of internet browser.

Additional important tips include:

• Have the form send email receipts to those who submit their email address

• Have a box donors can check to subscribe to your electronic newsletter

• Have a box donors can check if they want their donation to remain anonymous

• Once the form has been submitted, it should take the donor to a confirmation page that provides a printable donation receipt for their taxes

• Have a wide variety of amount boxes to check and a box where they can simply type in an amount

• Don't forget to send personal, handwritten thank you cards to large donors

The costs associated with accepting credit and debit cards online vary, so shop around. These costs may include set up fees for your site, transaction fees for each donation, and site maintenance fees. Your website administrator may be able to manage this tool, or you may have to hire an outside firm. Shop around for good deals and donated services. With the use of free tools like Google Analytics, you can track where donors and other site visitors come from and further promote your website on those search tools.

16. HONORARY DONATIONS

Many individuals like to give the gift of a charitable donation to a great cause. Etiquette experts consider it the thing to give the person who has everything. By creating website tools that allow users to donate in someone's honor for a specific cause, you dramatically increase your online donations. The organization gets a donation. The giver gets a tax deduction, and the recipient gets to know that they helped support a cause they believe in. It's a win-win-win!

Some organizations even have e-cards that can be customized for the recipient. There are some upfront and ongoing technology costs associated with the e-cards. However, offering 5 different basic cards can dramatically increase the number of donations of this kind you receive. An organization that has done a great job with this in the past is St. Jude's Children's Hospital. You should also offer to mail a card for a premium for large donations. This should be something a person must opt into on the website. The e-card and the traditional card should both include the text, "A donation has been made in your honor." Remember that offering this service helps you identify stakeholders, too. You receive the contact information of both the donor and the recipient in the process. Don't forget to thank the donor and offer both parties an opportunity to subscribe to your newsletter and donate in the future.

17. Individual Membership

Selling a membership in your organization is a great way to promote it, as well as to raise funds. Offering membership creates a long term personal relationship with those who identify themselves with your organization. One of the most famous and successful adopters of this fundraising method is National Public Radio. They have cultivated a system where they encourage donations at any level, but have a threshold for membership. With membership, donors get "thank you" gifts. If you give past the membership level at various increments, the value of your thank you gift increases.

This is a great model that I encourage other nonprofits to adopt. The key to it is setting the membership at a financially attainable level for the majority of your supporters. That varies significantly based on the geographical area, as well as the organization's stakeholders. For WBEZ Chicago Public Radio, membership is $120 per household annually. Thanks to automated payment plans, this level makes donating affordable to the majority of listeners. Keep in mind that some organizations, like radio, have no incremental costs when they add a consumer/client the way that a direct service provider does. As a result, they do not have to calculate an individual's cost into their membership price. Set your donation levels from very low to very high and allow for online donors to fill in an "other" box, too.

Acquiring thank you gifts is a challenge. First, go to your supporters and see if any of their businesses or business relationships will provide you with donated services or discounts to members. Second, look for at-cost options where businesses will donate the mark-up on a product. Finally, if all else fails, buy wholesale. Buying wholesale is a challenge if you are new to memberships because you will have to estimate the size of the order you need. In most wholesale orders, the volume affects the per piece cost. This encourages over-buying. If you must purchase wholesale and you do not know what your demand will be, commit to a thank you gift long term so you do not have to fear wasting products and money.

Send annual reminders at the 11 month mark and again at the 12 month mark if subscribers have not yet reviewed their membership. Include information about the services your organization has provided the community in the last year. To avoid the cost of postage and printing, try to enroll your members in automatic renewal via their credit or debit cards. If they decline this service, send your initial renewal request via email. Remember not to send too many emails or your supporter may mark you as spam or block you altogether.

18. BUSINESS OR ORGANIZATIONAL MEMBERSHIP

Associations, chambers of commerce, development groups, coalitions, and lobby groups all use business or organizational memberships. They raise funds and help legitimize your organization by associating it with prominent names.

Setting the price of this type of commercial membership is a challenge. I had success as Executive Director of a business association with membership levels set depending on the annual income of the business. This made membership attainable for small sole proprietorships, but still held large holding companies accountable for donating in proportion to their ability to pay.

Setting a value proposition for businesses or organizations can be a challenge. If a membership is tax deductible, make sure to prominently display this information. Provide members with discounted admissions to organizational events, as well as to events of partner organizations. Attempt to negotiate bulk buying or service discounts for items that are expensive for your members or that they use frequently. Remember that businesses are much like individual donors. They need to be reminded of the good you are doing in the community, the value of their donation in supporting that work, and what benefits they receive by donating.

19. Sponsorship

For most nonprofit organizations, sponsorships are an essential way to cover overhead costs. You can structure your sponsorships as annual commitments. I have found that having sponsorships tied to specific events encourages donations from smaller businesses, thereby increasing the number of potential sponsors. It also decreases your charities tie to one particular corporation, thereby reducing the chance that a consumer who has a poor view of a company might in turn have a poor view of your charity because it is sponsored by that company.

Consider the same price point and value proposition issues with sponsorship that you would consider with a business membership. I structured memberships for a major national foundation's largest annual event as:

Silver Level for donations of $250 - $499 | Benefits include:

• Logo on event website that is linked to company webpage

• Logo on the back of t-shirt given to all attendees at event

• Free event t-shirt mailed to sponsor

• Receipt for tax-deductible donation letter sent to company when check was received

• Hand written thank you card from director

• Listing of company's name in event program

• Opportunity to put promotional item in goodie bag

Gold Level for donations of $500 - $999 | Benefits include:

• All Silver Level benefits

• Larger listing of company's name in event program with website, phone number, address, and email

• Company's name and website on bookmark in goodie bag

Platinum Level for donations of $1000 or more | Benefits include:

• All Silver Level benefits

• All Gold Level benefits

• Larger listing of company's logo and name in event program with website, phone number, address, and email

• Company's name and website and address on bookmark in goodie bag

• Company's name, website, and phone number in 15 eNewsletters to participants and one general newsletter

• Company thanked in announcements at event

Do not forget the value of in-kind donations. You can turn a small event into a world class gathering with the benefit of in-kind donations. At an event I organized, I paid a total of about $20K for services and received about $100K in in-kind donations. The event brought in over $350K, giving the organization $330K in profits. It would have been $230K in profits if it wasn't for companies giving us services in exchange for sponsorships. This was a significant difference to this organization, whose annual international income is $4 million.

When reviewing potential sponsors, consider the image and activities of the company as it relates to your organization. I worked with a forest preserve on an event and as sponsorships came rolling in, we were conscious of the environmental impact of each potential sponsor. We did not waste time pursing sponsorships with oil companies. We knew we would not want them affiliated with the organization because it would negatively affect the forest preserve's brand.

Consider working with sponsorship brokerage companies if you are planning a large event or if your organization is prominent in the community. These firms are in the business of negotiating between large corporations and organizations to secure sponsorship deals. Brokers are often used for sports teams, sports events like marathons, or other televised or widely attended gatherings. Brokers should be honest and dependable. They should focus on making a deal that is of mutual benefit for the organization and for the corporation. Interview a broker carefully to make sure they are a good partner for the organization before committing to work with them.

20. CRA FUNDS

Community Reinvestment Action Funds, or CRA Funds, are money that banks are required to give out. The laws for CRA Funds continue to change. Banks give these funds to nonprofit organizations in low income communities that have not received the same proportion of loans as other communities. To comply with the complicated legislation that monitors these nonprofit contributions, financial institutions hire CRA Officers who administer these funds. This is typically a Vice President or Chief CRA Officer level position. Each institution has a different application system for these funds. Find out who the CRA officers are in all area financial institutions and then speak with them about how to apply for their CRA Funds. I had a lot of luck starting with a small request for only a few thousand dollars to get onto their annual giving cycle, and then increasing the amount each year.

21. RAFFLE

Raffles are a fun way to supplement any event. They also work on their own if you have a big enough prize to give away. Have stakeholders purchase the tickets they are selling. This way, if they lose the tickets or the ticket stubs, you do not have a major issue on your hands. Sell the tickets at a price that will really move them, such as $1 per chance or 11 tickets for $10.

Special things about raffles to keep in mind:

• In many raffles, sellers offer a deal based on the price of an arm's length of tickets. This disenfranchises women, the major demographic of nonprofit contributors.

• Most municipalities have regulations on raffles. They usually entail purchasing a raffle license and completing some paperwork in advance.

• Have the drawing of the winner in public and by a person not entered to win. If you are not doing the drawing at an event, have it at the office. You can invite stakeholders to be present.

• Remember, as with any nonprofit fundraiser, it is always a bad idea to purchase what you will be giving away. You do not want to be in the business of selling raffle tickets. You want your stakeholders to sell raffle tickets for you to supplement the association's income and not to dig you out of a hole dug by purchasing the prize. When you purchase prizes, you are gambling with your nonprofit's money, and that is not a gamble anyone can afford to take.

22. LONG SHOT HOOPS COMPETITION

A long shot hoops competition is one where individuals shoot a basketball from the 3 point line towards the opposite basketball hoop. Some competitions actually require an individual to throw it backwards over their head, too.

Whatever the case may be, usually participation begins by selling raffle tickets. Then, the present individuals with the winning one or two tickets are immediately invited down to shoot the basket. The numbers of tries they get are made clear in advance. So is the prize. Usually a maximum of three shots are given each winner, and a typically there are two winners.

Typical prizes include automobiles. However, you do not need to purchase a car. Simply purchase special event insurance that covers the possibility that someone might win a car. That insurance will pay out in the event of a winner and provide the car to them. The insurance company may have special regulations, including having a member of their team present during the competition. To entice people to purchase raffle tickets, ask a local car dealership to park a vehicle outside in a prominent location. Post a sign on it that says, "Win This Car! Buy a Raffle Ticket for Your Chance to Shoot & Win!" Having a car present is a great advertisement for the dealership and it turns the abstract idea of winning a car into a tangible reality: you could be driving that car right there. To make the event more fun, make sure you have an extroverted announcer who double-checks all the ticket numbers.

23. WINE TASTING

A wine tasting is a simple and elegant event. Simply contact local wine retailers and wineries and ask them to organize a wine tasting, or a series of tastings, for your donors. Schedule them at convenient times like Saturday and Sunday afternoons. Sell seats at the wine tastings to supporters.

At the event, offer them literature about your organization and snacks such as bread, crackers, grapes, figs, pistachios, cheese, and chocolate. Work with the wine shop to pair great snacks with the wines. Make sure that this tasting is in some way distinct from what is normally offered at a tasting. It can distinguish itself through the treats you offer, the wines tasted, and the fact that the winery won't be charging them—you will. Some wineries have free live music a couple of days a week, so pairing the time of the tasting to end right before the live music begins is a simple way to add to the experience for your attendees without adding to your cost.

24. LADIES BRUNCH

I have had the pleasure of organizing multiple ladies brunches. They are a great way to raise funds and hold a networking event to promote businesses. They are especially valuable to your organization if it targets women, and especially valuable to the attendees if it serves the business community.

Speak to local restaurants, catering companies, food manufactures, and grocery stores about donating items to the event. Many will happily put together platters and spreads for you to pick up and serve at the event. I have had lots of luck with women-owned restaurants who were eager to donate a spread and attend. Pick up goodies the day before, and handle food appropriately to prevent spoiling. You do not want to rush around the morning of the event, so leave that time available for setting up.

Depending on the level of involvement your supporters have, it may be possible to charge for this event and get attendees. I invited women to attend for free to encourage participation, but then sat out a donation tin and sign that said, "Suggested donation $5" with donation receipts. I also included in the invitation a note stating, "RSVP appreciated but not required." This encouraged people to commit to attending.

At the event I organized, a founder of the organization spoke briefly about the organization's activities, and the rest of the time was open for mingling. I played some soft classical music in the background. Attendees reported having a great time and some wanted to have another brunch as soon as the next week. While the event did not serve as a major fundraiser, it did further cultivate relationships with our donors and their friends and family. This is an important part of the long term financial stability of an organization. We made a few hundred dollars thanks to free food and space, and were able to touch base with our many of our most committed and loyal supporters.

25. BINGO!

Bingo is a fun fundraising event with very little overhead or organization required. You can purchase a bingo set, rent it, or create your own. It makes sense to rent it if you are only going to hold the event once. If it will be a reoccurring activity, then you should consider buying or getting donated the pieces you need from an amusement supply shop. You can buy the whole bingo setup from places like Doolin's Party Supply for $60.

Charge for each card individuals use to play and set prices based on the number of cards in play during a game. Typically, cards are $5 each for an hour of play. At the end of each hour, each participant has to re-buy their cards or return them for new ones. Confirm winners before having cards cleared. Some municipalities require licenses for bingo games, so check with your local government before organizing a bingo night.

Make sure you have some form of a sound system, so that all attendees can hear the announcements of letters and numbers. This will keep from you having to repeat yourself. Call each letter and number combination three times to allow adequate time for individuals to find it. For example, "B 12, B as in Boy, 12, B12". The more cards people buy, the longer they will need to check all of them off.

26. CAKE WALK

A cake walk is a fun game where participants pay to play. Then they move around from position to position marked on the floor. Each position is a cut out of a different color in the shape of a cake. Each cut out has a number on it, and it is taped securely to the ground. The caller plays music and participants move around from position to position. To keep people flowing there should be at least one empty space when you start. When the music is turned off, everyone stops on a spot. Then, the caller draws a number from inside a bowl. The winning number is the winner and gets the cake.

To play again each participant will have to pay again. The trick to making this a success is charging about $3 - $5 per person, having a cake donated that looks very appetizing, and not beginning the game until you have at least 10 contenders. The more participants you have, the more money you will make on each cake. Cakes with chocolate or yellow frosting and embellishments like flowers work great to get a crowd of interested participants.

This event works great at festivals. Announce it frequently over the intercom and have the caller invite passersby to participate while you are waiting to fill up. Then, make sure the music is something lively and loud that participants will likely dance to, such as "The Chicken Dance" or the "Hokey Pokey." This will draw attention and a crowd of people to compete next. At one event, we positioned this game on the stage of a gymnasium full of events. That way, when participants moved around and were awarded cake everyone could see and participation built throughout the event.

27. FACILITY TOUR

If the nonprofit organization has an office or other facility, a tour may be a great way to inform the public about your work and raise funds. If you have a manufacturing facility or other industrial building, check with your liability insurance before pursuing this type of event. Great candidates for this fundraiser are places that produce unique things, from public television stations to social entrepreneurships.

I once organized an event at an organization that manufactures candles. The candles paid for the career training that the employees and other community members received. Having community members walk through the area when production was closed, meet some of the employees, and learn about the organization by experiencing it increased attendees' support for the organization dramatically. Attendees wanted to donate more and purchase more goods from the organization, and some even signed up to volunteer.

A great tour provides attendees with the opportunity to see things the public can't normally see, meet people they can't normally meet, and get things they can't normally purchase. It also offers tickets for sale in advance and provides food and drinks. A tour should not be rushed; it should be more like a constant meander with frequent opportunities for questions, as well as talk amongst the group. Tour guides should be social, outgoing, attentive, accommodating, and informative. It's okay if a guide for an annual tour uses notecards. However, if the tours become weekly, your guides should memorize their presentations. Remember that, as with all events, clearly marked signs for the restroom are essential.

28. IN-KIND GIFTS

An in-kind donation is a donation of a good or service that is received for free instead of having to be purchased. Fundraising is hard work. Don't waste your proceeds by spending on things another vendor would give you for free. Some donations I have been able to wrangle include food, drinks, advertisements, production costs, vehicle rental, office space, postage, office supplies, copies, bus tickets, accounting services, moving truck rental, sound equipment, bands performing, payroll services, baby food, mailbox services—the list goes on and on. Many people want to give large checks to charities but cannot afford to. It is much more manageable to work for free or donate supplies. You would be surprised how many people and companies are happy to do so.

Look at where you are spending money currently. Are there services that you are currently paying for that could be donated to you? A great place to start is with payroll and accounting services. Office space can be procured through religious organizations or developers looking to fill in new projects until they have paying renters. A large and well-known real estate developer once donated office space to me for two years, as long as I did not tell anyone else about the gift. He did not want to be bombarded with requests. If you have cleaning or landscaping companies come in, consider whether it would be possible to instead use volunteer groups, such as an area horticultural club or work with the local probation office to get individuals performing mandatory community service to clean the offices after hours.

Another area that can be expensive for non-profits is energy costs. Ask area hardware stores to donate light sensors that only turn on lights when people are in areas. This is especially helpful with restrooms. If you cannot get the sensors, simply posting a sign asking for the lights to remain off can make a difference. Use contact paper to laminate the sign to make it look more official and to prevent having to replace it frequently. While you are contacting hardware and other home stores, also ask for water-saving units for your toilet tanks. If you are not comfortable taking on these type of projects yourself, considering asking a local service or construction company to donate a few hours of winterizing. If you pay your own utilities, this will help you save a bundle over the years. A great website for energy saving tips and techniques is www.energysavers.gov.

29. POLICY EVALUATIONS

Many nonprofits suffer from too few staff doing too much work for too little pay. This creates high turnover, which costs in organizational morale, productivity, overtime, and human resource costs. Determine which policies and procedures you can either remove altogether or streamline to lighten the employees' loads. If you cannot justify maintaining an employee full-time but need him or her 20 hours per week, look to partnering with similar organizations to share staff with you. Busywork wastes staff time and even the time of salaried staff costs you money.

Opportunity cost is lost when an employee highlights every work call on their mobile phone bill. Not only are they spending work time doing a frivolous chore, but they could be using that same time to improve your organization or provide service to your clients or your community. Instead, consider what is the purpose of this policy? How could its goals be more efficiently and respectfully achieved? Then, move forward with a decisive action. Remember that any change, no matter how much of an improvement, creates nervousness with many employees, so look for their input in the beginning, middle, and end of all transitions.

30. SEMINARS

Is your organization led by any industry leaders, inventors, unique thinkers, or dynamic speakers? If so, holding a seminar or series of seminars might provide you with a great fundraising opportunity. Many nonprofit organizations were founded by or have board members who are industry innovators. Organizing speaking engagements for them where their speaking fee goes to the organization is a simple way to bring in extra funds. Many universities, professional associations, and chambers schedule frequent speaking events throughout the year.

Leveraging the talents of your leadership can provide you with a forum to promote your organization, as well as an opportunity to make easy money on just a few hours of their time and attention. Remember to promote the event in your organization's newsletter and e-newsletter, press releases, website calendar, Facebook page, Twitter account, and any other way that you communicate with the community as a whole. This will provide an extra value to the organization or business that hires your leader as a speaker. Remember that most speaking fees vary depending on the size of the audience, the forum, and the type of organization the event is for. Travel expenses should always be covered by, and often are arranged by, the organization or business hiring the speaker.

31. TRAINING

Is your organization known for its strong position on the environment? Do you support kosher diets? Do you encourage peace education? If you have a unique market position on anything, then you can construction training around that. For instance, if your nonprofit organization promotes conservation, you can construct a training program for individuals on how to conserve. If your organization promotes fair trade, you can teach the public what fair trade means and how to shop fair trade. Remember when planning trainings that individuals tend to be available on Saturdays starting at about 10 am, and individuals attending as part of their professional work as businesspeople tend to be available from 9 to 4, Monday through Friday.

To legitimize your training, prepare an outline, handouts, and a presentation. Make it interactive. Have the facilitator rehearse the entire training at least once before it is offered. Consider the length of the training, and set the price at a level appropriate for what is being offered. Professional trainings take longer, are more technical, and are paid for by companies; as a result, they can cost more per participant. Remember that attendees will expect coffee in the morning and food at lunch or dinner time. A great addition to any training program is a certificate of completion signed by the most senior person in your organization

32. INDIVIDUAL CERTIFICATIONS

Organizations that hold expert positions in a field, even if it is just locally, are a great source for offering certifications. If your industry already offers some credentialing program, see if your organization can offer certifications in it. If your industry doesn't, get started creating one! A great way to get begin is to get all of your team members certified and then create strategic partnerships with other associations in the field that can also provide training for your certification.

An example would be: if your agency is an association that promotes peace through dialogue, you could offer a certification called "Certified Nonviolent Mediator." This could be exam-based, or simply conferred after completing a training program. Remember that individuals participate in training programs for personal and professional development, so titling your certification with a résumé-ready name is essential. "Certified Peace Dude" on a résumé will not help someone get a future job or promotion.

If you are able to get your certification program to count towards community education units or credits for professionals in your field, it will greatly increase interest in the program. Promote the program through trade associations and online forums. Don't forget to give a physical certificate. Nice certificate paper that prints in a standard printer is available very inexpensively online or at your local office supply shop. It should be signed by the facilitator and signed in advance by the most senior person in your organization.

33. BUSINESS CERTIFICATIONS

Businesses do not just like certifications; they need them to help them promote their business. Your organization can fill this need. If you are an association of synagogues, you could offer a "Certified Kosher Kitchen" to businesses that paid an application fee and were found after inspection to be kosher.

Remember that businesses need to be able to promote themselves with your certification. That means that you need to:

• Create a clearly identifiable window decal for the business, including the year of certification

• Maintain consistent and clear standards of evaluation

• Provide a physical certificate to the business for their records

• Evaluate each location of a business separately

• Encourage the business to use the decal as a logo on their menu and website while they are certified

• Charge a fee that is small enough not to be prohibitive to small businesses but covers your expenses for staff time and travel, as well provides you with enough profit for it to be worth administering the program

34. Movie Screening

A movie screening is a fun social event that is easy to organize and promote. Most chain theatres will not donate theatre space or ticket revenues to charities. Instead, look for venues like university theatres or auditoriums, screenings rooms, or community theatres. Some public libraries even have auditoriums with screens. If your community is lucky enough to have an independently-owned movie theater, then speak to the owner about organizing a screening during an off time.

Selecting a film can be a challenge. You should watch the film a couple of times with at least one other organization stakeholder to determine if it is appropriate for your organization to screen. Keep in mind when you select a film that your organization's name will be on a press release with the name of the film.

Most films do not let you legally screen them for profit without paying the film's production and/or distribution company. A great way to get around this red tape is to screen an independent film. In my experience, it has been very easy to contact the producer or rights owner of independent films through the film's website.

Schedule the film screening on a weekend. Matinees are good for family films. A nice 11 am film screening will allow for maximum family attendance. If children are welcome, say so publicly.

Sell tickets in advance and at the door. A great online service for pre-sales is www.brownpapertickets.com. It is free to nonprofit organizations, and includes a small fee for the individual who purchases the ticket. If you use Brown Paper Tickets' service, I recommend that you do not opt for paper tickets and just have people's names checked off a list at the door. Remember to keep prices low if you are looking for a family crowd.

Sell drinks and snacks at the event. If you cannot get them donated, go to buying clubs like Costco and get boxes of snack packs of chips, candy bars, and other treats. If your organization has boosters, ask them to make treats to sell instead. Cans or bottles of sodas and water are a must. You will be surprised how much of your profit comes from the snacks.

35. Selling Services

Take a long, hard look at your organization. Is there a service you offer your clients that you could be selling to the larger community?

If you provide free budget and debt services to low income households, you could charge individuals who do not qualify for your free services for the same advice and assessments that you are already providing. By selling services, you expand your stakeholder and client base.

This idea also takes advantage of the opportunity to earn extra income without large increases in overhead. The infrastructure exists. The unit cost is the only element affected. As a result, calculating the cost to your organization of selling additional or new services is easily done. Furthermore, setting a cost to the public will be easy because once you determine the market rate, you can assess if the profit margin from your unit costs makes pursing the sale of the service a viable fundraising option for your organization.

36. Cooking Class

Cooking classes are a fun and interesting way to raise funds for an organization. Many premium grocery stores and high end restaurants have test and instruction kitchens. Ask them to donate a class to your cause. You can pre-sell tickets. Remember when setting the price to charge approximately the same rate as the venue usually charges for a comparable class. In my experience, prices range from free to $120 per person. Remember to mention in your sales pitch for tickets that attendees will get to eat the creations and that wine is included, and then include it.

Give a simple and event-appropriate thank you gift to attendees. For instance, present a wooden spoon with a ribbon attached to a card that says, "Thank You for Helping Us Feed the Hungry." A brightly colored spoon or spatula will be a constant reminder of your organization and the great time they had at your event.

These events are ideal date nights, so schedule them on Friday or Saturday evenings. Like all public events, they should be scheduled at least 6 weeks in advance to allow for press coverage.

If you are unable to find a venue that usually holds these classes to donate a class to your organization, consider using a commercial or catering kitchen for the event and asking a local restaurant chef to provide the instruction. A restaurateur may be eager for an opportunity to promote their establishment, experiment with new dishes, and support a charity through their talents. If you are having trouble finding a chef, see if any area chefs are selling a cookbook. They may want to participate and tie in a cookbook signing to the event.

The key to having a successful fundraiser is planning and little to no overhead costs. It is not valuable to pay for space, a chef, food, thank you gifts, staff time, administration, promotion, etc. You want to be able to price tickets at a reasonable price and have all sales money become funds for the organization.

37. Online Shop

Sell your merchandise on your website! While upfront and maintenance costs exist with any online venture, the benefit of an online shop cannot be ignored. Raise awareness and funds without a lot of administrative hassle for your already busy team members. Consider your internal technological capacity as well as outside vendors. Make sure your shop allows individuals to:

- Ship to a different address than the billing address

- Make donations and add donations to their shopping carts

- Indicate that an item is a gift and should not be sent with a receipt

- Include a gift message in the package

A t-shirt is the great American megaphone. Get your message on it and put it in an online shop. Have shirts available with logos and with witty sayings. Many cities offer a plethora of one-hour t-shirt printing options, so you do not need to keep a large inventory of shirts in stock to have them on your website. A simple, "I support wind energy" shirt might have that statement or simply a picture of a wind turbine on it. Whatever the message, make sure that your logo and color scheme are incorporated.

Bumper stickers are another great way to promote your organization and sell a lot of inexpensively produced goods. Remember to offer sincere, direct, and clever options but do not include any messages that are offensive or are not in tandem with the image of the organization that you are cultivating in the community.

Do not forget the sales tax. Remember that your tax exemption status means that your organization does not pay sales tax on the items it purchases. You will still have to charge sales tax on purchases made from you. However, your online store does not charge tax on direct charitable donations. If you are confused, get guidance from your information technology vendor when needed.

38. ESTATE SALE

Long-time supporters may leave their entire estate to your organization in the event that they pass without heirs. In the case of liquid assets, the transfer of ownership can be managed by an estate attorney. However, in the event that this donation includes the physical goods a person owns, you may be in the position of organizing an estate sale. Estate sales are similar to yard sales, except that they typically include all of the items in the home of a deceased person.

Using a professional to assess, inventory, and liquidate the estate is essential. As an undergraduate, I worked for a university archives that inherited the estate of a local collector. The archivist and her team of student workers were tasked with rummaging through all the items now owned by the university. For months, we cleaned depression-era china. When one of the students found part of a human skeleton among the boxes, the archivist instructed us to put it in the room for "potentially valuable goods." It wasn't until a Rembrandt etching was found that the archivist questioned the soundness of having students making minimum wage sorting and cleaning the goods.

Shop around for services to find places that offer auctioneer services as well as appraisal. Items remaining after auctions efforts are exhausted can be sold as large lots to resale shops or antique stores.

39. ICE CREAM SOCIAL

An ice cream social is a fun and informal way to raise funds. Ask local creameries to share their ice cream for free as a donation. If that tactic doesn't work, try to get it at cost. Make sure to get fixings, too. In my experience, holding this event in a school gymnasium works well. Toppings are a must. Plan to have a speaker to talk about your organization in an informal and unscripted manner. You can charge by the scoop with an extra fee to use the toppings. Set up a tip jar to tip for your cause. Servers should be in hairnets or hats, wearing gloves, and volunteering their time.

Remember that children are messy, so disposable bowls and spoons will help keep the event neat. At an ice cream social I planned, I received a donation of several cases of a local beer crafter's new blend. It seemed like a weird combination, but we ran out of beer before we ran out of ice cream. I offered the beers on a donation basis and was able to receive even more donations. By offering sorbet, I was able to provide a treat to the lactose intolerant, too.

40. BEER TASTING

Much like a wine tasting, a beer tasting is a simple, easy, and social way to raise funds. If you are lucky enough to operate in a community with numerous brew houses, you will have a great start list of companies to ask to host and donate beer to a beer tasting. Perhaps they would be willing to give your guests a private tour, too? If you cannot get a brew house to agree to the donation, then speak to a beer distribution company.

You should pre-sell tickets to the event and check IDs before the event begins. The event should open with a representative of your organization thanking attendees for their support and talking briefly about the cause. Then the facilitator should take over for the duration of the event. This will prevent the tone of the event from changing from social back to business.

The facilitator of the tasting is the key to the event being successful. This individual should be knowledgeable, engaging, and have a passion for beer. Hopefully, they work for the brewery or distributor. They should showcase unique brews not widely available to the public. Any tips given to the facilitator should go to the organization. This can be made clear through setting out a jar with a logo for the organization on it.

41. DUNK TANK

A dunk tank is a large tank of water with one transparent side. A person sits on the top. When a target is hit with a ball, the person falls in. Your organization sells chances to throw balls. I recommend selling them for $5 for three chances with three different balls. Make sure that the individual playing is far enough away from the target so that hitting it is possible, but not guaranteed.

The secret to the success of the dunk tank is having someone in the tank that people want to see dunked. This could be a prominent community member or politician. I have seen organizations hire local models to wear white t-shirts over bikinis. I find that the most successful dunkee is a clown in costume who teases players. This requires a very good-spirited clown. Have the individual managing the event collect money, hand out and collect the baseballs, and encourage participation from the crowd.

Tanks can be rented from party supply and amusement stores. You will need access to an outside water line to fill it with water. Have the tank delivered early because filling it will take a lot of time. This fundraiser works great as a part of other outdoor or gymnasium activities.

42. JUMP-A-THON

A jump-a-thon is a fundraising event where participants jump on small individual trampolines for a selected amount of time. When I participated in one of these events, it was 12 hours of jumping. We operated four trampolines with jumpers changing on at least one of the trampolines every half hour.

Jumpers were encouraged to get pledges to see how long they could jump. The real income came from holding the event by a widely used sidewalk and having a couple of dozen individuals with cans and matching t-shirts spread out and ask passersby for donations.

43. WALK-A-THON

Walk-a-thons are fundraisers where the participants walk for a very long time. This is frequently from 24 hours to a couple of days. These fundraisers offer the opportunity to raise funds with very little overhead. The most famous walk-a-thon in the nonprofit world is the Susan G. Komen Three-Day. However, your walk does not have to be that long. In fact, I've attend walk-a-thons that started at noon and ended at noon the next day. Each team could have up to 10 members. There was a track, and as long as one member of their team was always walking, they were still participating in the walk-a-thon. Participating team members were welcome to camp out in the event area. Donated entertainment was available at a stage throughout the entire 24-hour period. Each team was asked to raise at least $1000. More was encouraged. The event was held in donated park space, so the overhead cost was minimal. Each participant who raised $100 or each team that raised $1000 or more received a t-shirt.

44. MARATHON TEAM

A marathon team is a team of runners who run in a marathon to support a cause. They train for months or even years to prepare for the marathon. Individuals show their support of the runner and your organization by donating to it. Many marathons have sophisticated systems for registering charity running teams, so do your research before the marathon registration opens. While runners on your "team" train together and often wearing matching shirts during the race, they each run individually in the actual marathon and still have an individual running time.

Recruit marathon runners early. With any fundraiser, you should look first to your stakeholders for supporters. Then consider reaching out to the running community. When we organized a team for the Chicago Marathon, we had a lot of luck putting postcards in shoe stores and athletic apparel companies. We also attended special training days scheduled by the marathon to table and hand out information. These events were all organized by and managed by volunteers, so staff time was not an issue. As a result of their efforts, runners from as far away as Ireland were raising money for our cause. When the race was over, we thanked them by giving all runners who raised $500 or more a running shirt with our logo on it as a thank you.

The more runners you have, the more benefits marathon organizers offer you. As a result, this is the type of event that you should build on each year. If your area does not have a marathon race, then consider having a mini-marathon team. Mini-marathons are just slightly shorter marathons and are frequently available in medium and large cities. Remember to have all runners sign waivers of liability and get event insurance for this and every event your organization holds or participates in.

45. TRIATHLON TEAM

Having a triathlon team is very similar to having a marathon or mini-marathon team. Participants can be recruited from your stakeholders or from members of the community. Tri-athletes can also be recruited from events leading up to the event, as well as from gyms, athletic shops, and community centers. As a result of fewer tri-athletes in the community:

• Focus your recruiting efforts on individuals who were already planning on participating in the event.

• Provide great fundraising support to participants

• Try and organize other athletes and stakeholders to support the event by organizing a support team to staff cheering stations

46. WORLD RECORD CHALLENGE

Want to build excitement for an organization and get press coverage? Attempt to break a world record! Breaking the record is not as important as simply attempting it. Choose the record you are going to take on very carefully. Do not attempt to break any world records that:

• Are potentially dangerous or hazardous

• Humiliate or hurt participants

• Reflect poorly on the organization or on those who organized the event

I recently participated in a fundraiser that attempted to break the world record for number of jack-o-lanterns lit at the same time in the same place. An area city boosted tourism, business revenue, and morale when they charged participants per pumpkin to help carve up jack-o-lanterns. Crowds from surrounding communities eagerly paid $2.50 to carve a jack-o-lantern and be part of the world record attempt. Meanwhile, carvers also visited area businesses and purchased goods at tables the city rented out to vendors. The area was all atwitter for weeks about the attempt.

47. FACEBOOK PAGE

Everyone knows that Facebook is a popular way to connect with new and old friends. An easy way to reach out to the ever-growing Facebook nation is to create a charity page on Facebook with a donation button. Use the page to frequently announce events, activities, and accomplishments. Make sure that your administrative settings are set so that the email creator is an organization email that can be accessed in the event a team member leaves the organization abruptly.

48. TWEET-A-THON

Don't be a twit, tweet! A tweet-a-thon is a Twitter movement. You tweet that you are participating in a tweet-a-thon for your cause. Tell people you just donated and provide the website to them to donate. Then tell them to tweet when they've given, too. It becomes a chain letter of donations. This also promotes your organization to all the donors' followers.

49. HAUNTED HOUSE

A haunted house can raise funds for your organization if you are able to get the location donated and the actors to give their time. Creating a scary and safe event can be a challenge. Look for help partnering with community members with theatre backgrounds. If your organization is a theatre company, then be prepared for attendees to have very high expectations for the event. $10 is a typical haunted house entry charge. Remember that waivers of liability and warnings about scares are essential.

50. ARCHITECTURE TOUR

An architecture tour is a great fundraiser because of its incredibly low overhead. A walking tour of a historic neighborhood provides a leisurely and interesting Saturday or Sunday afternoon. Sell tickets in advance and before the start of the tour. Advertise at community places where retirees and culture and architecture enthusiasts frequent. Promote it to tourists, too. Include public and private libraries. It is ideal to start and end the tour at the same location. This should be a public place, and ideally the first place you discuss on your tour.

Have your tour guide do research and have information cards prepared about each location. They should do at least one practice walk-through with other team members or volunteers. The tour guide can use note cards to keep the facts about each site clear in their mind. I would plan the tour for 2 pm on Saturday and Sunday. If there is enough interest for more tours, then schedule morning tours on Saturday and Sunday as well. If this event draws consistently large crowds, then consider having a tour guide who receives a stipend for their time and memorizes their remarks. Also, consider expanding to sell your merchandise.

51. HISTORICAL SITE TOUR

The fundraising model for a historical site tour is similar to that for an architecture tour. The keys are to sell tickets in advance, to have a tour guide donate their time, and to provide food. Promote this event at typical cultural sites as well as to history clubs and interest groups. Remember history majors and scholars when looking for potential ticket buyers.

52. Historic Site Crawl

If your area historical sites are too far apart to make up a walking tour, consider having a historical site crawl. Volunteers in period attire at each site can interact with participants as if they have traveled in their own cars through time. You will likely need permission for this event from area historical societies, town officials, and/or parks departments.

At each site, volunteers collect donations for your cause. Do not charge per location, but simply ask for a suggested donation on the sign. Make sure that signs clearly explain to visitors what is happening and what other locations are participating. This will keep your characters from having to try and explain your charity and the event while staying in character.

This event is fun and encourages participation from many community members who might not have been interested in a walking tour. See if your local reenactment clubs will help you bring this event to realistic life. Help might also be found at community theatre groups. Theatres' costuming departments may be helpful in creating a memorial event.

53. Historical Reenactment

An historical reenact appeals to individuals who would be interested in attending a historical tour, as well as tourists and theatre goers. Work with area theatre companies, reenactments groups, and historical societies to plan the event. If possible, schedule the event on the anniversary of a historical event in your area. Sell tickets in advance and also sell tickets, concessions, and memorabilia at the event.

54. Craft Fair

A craft fair is a great event if your organization has a large group of local and craft volunteers. Schedule the event before the holiday season. Ask each committee, class, or other division to make goods to sell. If possible and appropriate, have clients make goods, too. Remember, with crafts, the goods can cost more than the retail costs of the finished product, so use supplies that you can acquire inexpensively. If you need help, there are lots of great online craft sites, including marathastewartliving.com.

At the event, play music to encourage shoppers to linger. Consider incorporating a bake sale. Remember to set up your sale in a high traffic and highly accessible area. If you have weather concerns, have the main event inside with street vendors selling food and drinks outside to help get people to attend. Crowds bring crowds.

55. SPEED NETWORKING

Speed networking is becoming an incredibly popular event. The concept is simple: you match up professionals in similar-interest industries. Everyone pays to attend. At the event, the professionals progress through their matches and meet 6 to 8 people for 10 to 15 minutes each.

There are services you can hire to arrange the event, but one organized professional could do it themselves. Have individuals RSVP for the event via a free web survey like surveymonkey.com. On the registration, they should identify their industry and the top three industries with which they would like to meet, in order. If you cannot accept payment in advance online, encourage individuals to mail checks in advance. Make sure they are aware of a no refund policy. Also accept payment at the event. Typical charge is $10 or $20 - $25 if a drink and appetizer is provided. Cut the registration off far enough in advance allow you to have time to match up all the professionals. Make sure everyone has a match for each session, even if it is not someone in their top three industries.

At the event, set up table tents with location numbers and have a letter on each side. For instance, the first place two people might sit would have a table tent that on one side said Table 1, Position A and on the other said Table 1, Position B. While people check in for the event, allow them some space for informal networking. Each person should receive a card with their matches and locations. For instance: April Jervis, Session 1: Table 3, Position B, Sara Smith, Session 2: Table 7, Position A, John Anderson, etc. On Sara Smith's card, it will show her she has Session 1 at Table 3, Position A with April Jervis. If an individual's match does not show up to the event, have a specific place for individuals without matches to go so they can spend that time networking with the other individuals whose matches are not there for that session.

You will need to explain to everyone how speed networking works before the event starts. Make sure to remind attendees to exchange business cards and allow time for each person to speak. Tell them the amount of time they have with each match. Do not forget to thank attendees for their support of your organization and for its importance in your community. Allow for a small amount of informal networking time at the end of the event.

56. Formal Dinner

Formal dinners are a challenge for fundraising experts because they entail many overhead costs that are hard to get donated. An organization can spend a fortune on a venue, food, entertainment, advertising, and staff time and end up losing a lot. I have known organizations to have to lay off staff after a formal dinner fundraiser. Before planning this event ask yourself the following questions:

- Do my stakeholders want to attend a formal dinner?

- Are they able and willing to pay $50 a plate or more for food and drinks?

- Are there enough of them in the local community to sell out seats at the event?

- Is this the best use of staff and volunteer time?

- What are the actual costs to holding this event?

- Can we realistically make back our expenses?

- Do we have the cash or credit available to cover the event's costs until we receive income from the event?

- Who can we depend on to buy tickets?

- Are there organizational boosters, member groups, supporting associations, or individuals we can depend on to buy a table of seats?

Presuming the answers to these questions have led you to plan this event, you should start with a budget. How much money can you afford to lose if this event is a bust? Speak to area venues and catering companies to see if any of them will provide you with a meal at a deep discount. Often the cheapest option is to get a space donated and then bring in an outside caterer to offer you a deal. You may be able to get a catering company to charge you very little over costs for the food and servers.

I recommend bringing in your own alcohol and volunteer bartenders. Have bartenders dress in all black, including a black tie. Each table should be round and should have a bottle of white and a bottle of red wine. Then, purchase inexpensive alcohol for bartenders to serve from one or two bar locations, depending on the size of the event. A basic bar should include vodka, gin, whiskey, orange juice, cranberry juice, tonic water, olives, maraschino cherries, and stirrers/straws. All drinks should be a standard price, such as $5 per drink, and the tip jar should be clearly labeled as for the organization. If possible, use disposable cups. Bartenders should only accept cash.

Entertainment, such as a band, should be donated for the event. Sound should be donated, too. You should ask your sound company to play music when the band isn't playing. Some bands have the ability to do this for you.

Remember to plan articulate and passionate speakers to thank attendees, remind everyone of the importance of the organization, and invite them to make additional donations with the donation cards handed out to each attendee. If possible, incorporate auctions or other activities into the event. Have organizational founders, board members, and directors attend and mingle.

57. AWARDS BANQUET

A simple way to turn a formal dinner into a publicized community event is to make it an awards banquet. Create prestigious awards and give them out at the banquet. For instance, a women's group I am a member of gives out an annual "Woman of the Year" award. They have a volunteer search committee find the winner each year. You should also use the event to thank volunteers by giving out certificates to board members. Consider also giving out a "Fundraiser of the Year" award to the volunteer who raises the most money for the organization throughout the year. Do not give out more than a couple of awards, or they will be devalued.

The event should be structured with a speaker talking about the organization and introducing the other speakers. Someone should prepare a speech about the award and the recipient. The winner should not be surprised about the award. They should be in attendance to accept it and give a prepared speech about their work in your field. The program should conclude with a call to action to attendees. Remember to have printed programs available for everyone. They should include brief biographies of all the speakers, a schedule of the speakers, a thank you to board members, and a thank you to event sponsors. In the past, I have had luck getting print companies to donate the programs in exchange for sponsorship.

This event should be an annual event that builds on its past success each year. Award winners should attend for free with a guest but everyone else should buy a ticket just like with a formal dinner fundraiser.

58. Street Festival

A street festival is a great way to raise a little money, get lots of press, and promote businesses in a particular area. This fundraiser is especially appropriate if you are a street association or chamber of commerce. Get permits to close the street well in advance. Choose a street where the majority of area businesses want to participate. In my experience, these events boost business primarily in restaurants and bars, so clothing or other retail shops might not be as excited to have the event on their street. The street should also be very walkable and clean with parking available on adjacent streets. Streets that typically get a lot of sidewalk traffic are a great pick.

The festival should be scheduled at least a year in advance. Choose a weekend when there a not a lot of competing events in the area. Summers are great, but try to avoid scheduling in the thick of heat.

You will need to rent port-o-potties. I have found that companies will not provide them for free to nonprofit organizations, but some will waive pick up and drop off fees and discount the prices. Make sure you get at least one wheelchair accessible port-o-potty. Speak to the vendor to see if they will be providing toilet paper and instant hand sanitizer. Some events will require buying extra of both. Speak to your municipality about when pick up of the portable toilets must be completed. Some cities will allow the portable toilets to remain on site after the event for up to 24 hours, and some will not.

The festival should feature area bands. Some bands may be willing to donate their time and talents for your event. However, most bands that are established enough to bring a crowd will likely expect to be compensated for their time.

You will also need stage and sound services. Your stage vendor may also be able to provide you with temporary walls to rope off the street at both ends. You may be able to negotiate for free stage and wall rental if the company provides you with tables, chairs, and small tents for vendors.

Pre-sell table and tent space to vendors. Provide discounts for early rental and for nonprofit organizations. I recommend creating a vendor application form that you provide on your website in pdf format. Bring it in person to area businesses to invite them to participate. Do not forget to get copies to all the businesses on adjacent streets.

See if the area chamber of commerce will send information about it out to their members. Use their online website to get a directory of all area businesses, then email the pdf to all of them. Let them know that they are invited to be part of your exciting event. As the event gets closer, follow up with businesses that have not yet responded, and let them know when registration is getting close to ending. Send an email with a subject line like, "2 Spaces Left for Main Street Fest!"

Have volunteers work the entry ways the day of the event. They should sell admittance. Young children should be free. Have a way of identifying those 21 and older, such as a hand stamp. Keep the entry price low to encourage attendance.

After the event, remember to clean up before leaving. When you get back to the office, send thank you notes to vendors, sponsors, bands, volunteers and other supporters who made the event successful.

59. BLOCK PARTY

A block party is very similar to a street festival. However, it is often organized by residents' associations or other community groups and held in areas like cul-de-sacs, community gardens, intersections, parks, or other areas where people can congregate into clusters. Because of the grouping up of attendees in a concert-like environment, band selection is very important. Consider having area dance troops perform. You may also want prominent community members to speak. Have vendors arranged in a circle around the outside perimeter.

60. Pub Crawl

A pub crawl is an event where a group of people walk from one point to another, stopping at bars along the way for drinks. If you are planning a pub crawl as a fundraiser, sell tickets in advance and before departing on the crawl. As part of the ticket price, provide each participant with an event t-shirt. This will help prevent you from losing members and help bartenders identify your group along the way.

Have each participating bar along the route give a sample drink of their "house specialty" to each crawl member. Allow enough time for individuals to buy and consume a full drink of anything they really like. Use a flag, silly hat, or other identifier to distinguish the pub crawl leader. Depending on the size and robustness of the group, the leader may also need a whistle and megaphone.

Remember that with any event involving alcohol, it is important to make sure the event is covered by your liability insurance, that those consuming alcohol are over 21, and that the event does not reflect poorly on the organization.

61. Dinner Crawl

A dinner crawl is similar to a pub crawl. Participants walk from restaurant to restaurant. At each place they get a small sample item that has been donated for the event. Make sure the menu is planned so it makes logical sense and ends with dessert. Participating restaurants will get:

• The opportunity to support a good cause

• A tax deductible donation

• To showcase their talents to individuals interested in dining out with a disposable income

• The chance to sell beverages to participants

To add class to this event, provide a program listing the name of each restaurant, the chef or restaurateur, the name of the dish being served, and a mouthwatering description of the dish. If you are really organized, collect photos of the dishes in advance and add them to the program, too.

You may want to have this crawl operate without a leader. Participants purchase tickets in advance or at the starting location and then do the crawl themselves at their own pace. They should all be given wrist bands to identify them to participating restaurants.

62. HOMEMADE DINNER CRAWL

A homemade dinner crawl is just like a standard dinner crawl, only each destination on the route is a volunteer's house. The volunteer shares dishes they have prepared.

The program you provide to participants has addresses and parking instructions instead of information about the chef. Just because someone wants to be host site does not mean their house works logistically for the event this year. Each host should have signs outside to help guide participants. Accessibility is the key with this event, so choose locations carefully. If you are lucky, they will be within walking distance.

Your program should have time ranges for each site, too. For instance: "Jervis Family, Soup Buffet, 5:00 – 8:00 pm, 123 Main Street, Somewhere, USA, Parking available on street." The next site should start 30 minutes later: "Smith Family, Salad Bar, 5:30 – 8:30 pm, 234 Main Street, Somewhere, USA, Parking available for free in public garage." Participants are not required to go to each location.

Tickets should be sold in advance or at the first site. Hosts will likely be eager to sell tickets to their friends and family to have familiar faces at their home for the event. Each site should have literature about the organization available. Music should play in the background to lighten the mood and remove the pressure to make constant conversation with strangers.

63. HOUSE PARTY

A house party is exactly what it sounds like: a party at someone's house. You charge for admission, play music on the sound system, and provide appetizers. It is about as simple an event as you can organize. I recommend having a volunteer organize it and hold it at their own house as a private third party event.

A simple way of tracking RSVPs for this type of event is a free online service like evite.com that allows you to create and send free invitations via email. It will track your RSVPs and help you promote the event by letting invitees invite their own guests.

64. DINNER PARTY

Dinner parties work well as third party events. Volunteers invite their friends and family. Ask all attendees to kick in $10 - $20. Then provide them with dinner and drinks. Everyone gets to enjoy each other's company and a little money is raised for the cause. In my experience, you can maximize the number of attendees by having two hosts for each dinner and by serving the meal as a buffet. Make sure hosts are aware of the risks to their carpets and lock up their valuables in advance.

To make this event even bigger, businesses have a different volunteer throw one of these for their contacts each month of the year, for a total of 12 parties. Provide an award at the end of the year for the individual that raises the most money and say thank you to all hosts. Added benefits of this event include:

• Strengthening the relationship that key donors have to the organization

• Spreading the word about the organization to additional community members

• Does not require the organization's resources or staff time

65. Mystery Dinner Theatre

A mystery dinner theatre is like a standard dinner party, only there is a mystery to solve. You can purchase mystery dinner kits that have the story and characters all prewritten for you. Some free samples are available online as well. Make sure you carefully review the mystery and its instructions before the event. At the event, players compete to try and solve the mystery of "who done it."

Pretending someone has been murdered is inappropriate. If the kit you order has a murder, rape, or other violent crime in it, exchange that element of the story for a much more humorous crime such as "who moved my cheese" or "who ate the last cookie."

These events can be fun and memorable. You are offering a special experience, so you can charge more for attendance. You can also make this an annual event that couples make a tradition.

66. Golf Outing

Golf outings are a challenge to organize for a nonprofit organization. The overhead costs are high and the time commitment and costs to participants are high as well. Aside from the typical costs of staff time and promotion for the event, you may find that some golf courses want to charge to rent out the facility and for each golfer to golf. That adds up quickly. The only way to reduce costs on an event like this is if you find a resort that will make a good deal with you. Ask for special rates at private courses, country clubs, and public courses.

To promote this event, leave fliers and postcards at sporting goods stores, golf courses, driving ranges, gymnasiums and other places athletic people may go. Contact all the area sporting clubs with an invitation. Send email and printed invitations to golf clubs and associations. Ask all appropriate groups to put your event in their newsletter and on their online calendar of events.

At the event, consider having volunteers work special holes, such as a marshmallow hole or left-handed hole. At an event I helped organize, we were able to get a car donated if anyone could make a hole-in-one of a particular hole. No one did, but having the car there added to the excitement of the event.

Food and drinks are important. At a recent golf outing, we organized a breakfast in the club house and then sold beverages at the 3,

6, and 12 holes. After the event, we gave a trophy to the person with the best score. We invited all participants to attend a dinner at the country club after the event for an additional charge.

67. LONGEST DRIVE COMPETITION

A longest drive competition is a golfing event where awards are given to the individual who hits the ball the furthest. An award should be given for the woman and the man who have the longest drive.

Hold the event at a driving range that has donated space for the day. This event should be promoted to the same groups as a golf outing. Try to get a basket of items donated for each winner from various area sporting goods stores. A trophy is a must, too. Make sure it has the year on it to provide an incentive for competitors to keep coming back even after they win.

All participants should pay to play and should get a certain number of drive attempts per pay. Sell food, drinks, and merchandise. Create a fun atmosphere that will make competitors' families come out to watch the competition and buy your hotdogs.

68. MATCHING FUNDS

Matching funds are donations that companies make to nonprofit organization to match the donations made by their employees. Many corporations, large and small, participate in matching programs. In fact, many of your current donations might qualify for matching funds. Ask donors to speak to their human resources departments about matching gift programs. Most simply require a one page form to be completed and signed by a representative of the nonprofit organization. There are online directories of large corporations with well-known matching programs that can be easily searched by donors.

69. FAMILY BOWLING

Bowling fundraisers are a social and informal way to raise funds. They work well for family-oriented organizations such as schools or religious charities. Participants pay to play. Getting lanes and shoe rentals donated is an attainable goal. The challenge will be convincing a bowling alley to let you bring in donated food to sell. You may also want to sell organizational merchandise, such as t-shirts, at the check in. If the volunteers working the table and arriving early are all wearing your t-shirts it will likely catch on with the rest of the attendees.

At a recent charity bowling event I attended, the organizers enhanced the event by providing awards such as "youngest bowler" and "best victory dance." It made the event more exciting for participants. Winners received family memberships to local museums that had been donated to the charity.

70. BOWLING COMPETITION

For the slightly more competitive crowd, a bowling competition might be the right fundraiser. Reach out to area leagues for participants. When scheduling this event, you may need to schedule it around league play to get participants. This may require you contacting all the area bowling alleys.

Competitors are divided into groups by age and each age group is given an award. Have the gutters covered for the children's game. Assemble mixed teams of four individuals with at least one person of each gender. This means a team can be one woman and three men, two women and two men, or three women and one man. If there is enough interest, add a singles competition, too.

Funds are raised on admittance fees and food and merchandise sold at the event. Consider having special event shirts made that display the name of the event and the year on them.

At the end of the event, thank all participants for their support of your organization. Thank the bowling alley for hosting. Thank all donors, including any who gave in-kind gifts such as trophies or prizes. Then, give out the awards starting with the children. Make sure that everyone has time to clap for each award winner.

71. COMEDY SHOW

Hold a comedy show. Sell tickets in advance and at the door. Offer a discount for advance purchase. Sell food and drinks at the event.

Getting a bar to operate for a day at a loss is very unlikely. Hold the event at another venue such as a cultural center, parks department building, or at the organization's office. In my community, the police department has a training room which many community organizations use for free.

When selecting a comedian, reach out to area universities, improvisation troupes, and other community comedy groups. They may be willing to donate their talents for the experience. Make sure you speak to all the performers about keeping the content clean.

To keep the mood of the event light, spare the audience a long speech about the organization's work. Instead, begin the show by saying thank you to attendees for supporting the organization and then introduce the first performer. Close with another thank you.

Have a volunteer or two sell merchandise at the back of the room before and after the event. Volunteers can sell the food and drinks too. This will keep overhead costs low.

72. KARAOKE NIGHT

This fundraiser is inexpensive and easy to organize. Renting a karaoke machine is typically $50 to $100. You may even be able to get one donated. Use a free space—this makes all the difference with this event. The event profit will be the sale of food and drinks throughout the night.

Dim the lights, welcome guests, and let the off-key fun begin. Get an extroverted M.C. to host the evening and recruit singers. Have volunteers sell food and drinks throughout the night. They should walk around the crowd taking orders like wait staff: this will keep people ordering all night long. At the end of the night when the volunteer brings the bill, make sure it includes a note saying that the funds received benefit the organization and any tips left will go to the organization, too.

73. PLAY

Organizing a play is a lot of administrative work. However, if the actors are donating their services, if the stage and lights are all donated, and if the venue is donated or greatly reduced in cost, then the play will be a source of fundraising income.

Try to get a theatre company to donate a performance to your cause. This saves a lot of administrative time and hassle in organizing the performance yourself. The benefit to the theatre company includes:

- Opportunity to support a good cause

- Opportunity to promote the theatre

- Free press coverage from your organization promoting the event

- Opportunity to showcase the company's talents to your organization's stakeholders

- Opportunity for a large tax deduction if the company is not a charity itself

After the performance, organize a panel discussion, reception, or other event to make the performance special. In my experience, having the fundraising performance be the first performance works well. That way the company can benefit from the hype during their continued run of the show.

Choose the play carefully. A play should be of interest to the organization's stakeholders and of interest to the general public. Read the play and attend a table reading of the play before the event to make sure it is appropriate. If possible, bring at least one other stakeholder with you to provide a second opinion.

Scheduling your showing as a matinee will mean the event will be very family-friendly. Have a reception afterwards with food and drinks. Ask stakeholders to buy and sell tickets through an easy-to-use online service. This event should have special tickets—not the same tickets used for normal showings at the theatre. Ask company members to mingle with attendees at the reception. Sell organizational merchandise at the reception. Also, set out nice donation cans around the reception buffet so that if an individual would like to make an additional donation, they are easily able to.

Do not price the tickets out of reach of potential attendees. They should cost slightly more than a normal show at the theatre because of the additional reception and/or discussion. Start selling early and focus on selling out.

74. MUSICAL THEATRE

A musical theatre production is the same type of fundraiser as a play. However, the production is a musical. Because of the lively nature of the event, panel discussions will not work as an after show activity. Receptions are a must. With permission from the playwright, sell song books as part of the merchandise at the reception. Autographed copies are all the better.

75. DINNER THEATRE

A dinner theatre event consists of a play that is performed while the audience enjoys dinner. This event allows you to charge more for tickets because it is providing guests with a full meal and entertainment. These events are typically set dinner menus with only the option of one of two possible main dishes. They work great on date nights, so matinees will not do as well in ticket sales. Do not forget to provide event information to all the cultural and event publications. Reach out to university theatre departments to encourage their students and faculty to buy tickets, too.

A typical theatre will not work for this event, so look for school or religious organizations' gymnasiums for venues. This will allow for a greater selection of possible performers because a troupe that is not affiliated with a specific venue can be brought in. In my experience, lively productions like musicals work best for this type of event.

Remember to provide programs that thank sponsors, provide information on the players, thank volunteers, and provide additional information about the organization, its accomplishments, and how to make a charitable donation.

76. CAR WASH

A car wash is a cheap and easy way to raise a little cash. Make sure your location is prominent and accessible. Get soap and scratch free sponges. Make sure you have access to unlimited water from a hose.

Schedule lots of volunteers to hold brightly colored signs and rotate through cleaning the cars. I recommend that you get black poster board and use white or neon letters to spell out "Car Wash" and the price per wash. Volunteers should wear matching t-shirts that clearly advertise the benefiting charity.

77. CAR DRY

A car dry is when a charity works with an automated car wash to dry vehicles by hand. This must be arranged with the owner of the automated wash. Volunteers hold signs indicating the cost of the wash and hand dry. Then, volunteers collect cash before vehicles enter the wash machine and hand dry the car when it exits. Make sure customers know that they are supporting your charity and that tips go to the charity, too. T-shirts and donation cards are necessary.

78. DEALERSHIP CAR WASH

Automotive dealerships hire companies to come in and wash all of their vehicles. Convince a local dealership to hire the organization's volunteers instead. The washing must leave each car spotless. Schedule volunteers in shifts so that no one person has to work more than four hours. In my experience, income from the event ranges from one thousand to several thousand dollars, depending on the number of cars and the generosity of the owner. This is all income thanks to volunteers donating their time.

79. CALENDAR

A calendar filled with photos of puppies and kittens makes a great fundraiser for animal shelters and other groups focused on animals. Puppies and kittens sell. Photographs of them are easy to take. Lots of online and physical office supply stores offer calendar services. They may even donate the calendars to the organization. Then, sell the calendars as the fundraiser. It works best to sell them in November, December, and January. It is hard to sell a print calendar for more than $20 per copy, so volume is the key to high returns. Put the calendars in a packet of five and sell them to stakeholders for $90 per pack, or $20 each.

80. A Year of Giving

A year of giving is a fundraiser where you look for a donor for each day of the year. Put a calendar online and on each day of the year, put the number of day it is in the year. For instance January 1st is the 1st day of the year and February 1st is the 32nd day of the year. Then using the online program, ask stakeholders to pick a day and donate the value of that day. The donor can choose to have the date on the online calendar say, "Donation made by April Jervis," "Anonymous," or "Donation in memory of Jane Smith." If you are able to get every calendar date in a year taken at $200/day, then you will raise a total of $73,000 in donations. This fundraiser has very low overhead costs, but requires a large donor base to be successful.

81. Paper Cut-Outs

Many nonprofit organizations use paper cut-outs to drum up donations. They find places of business like grocery stores, restaurants, or gas stations and ask each customer to donate $1 to the cause. If they do they are given a paper cut-out of something that ties into the cause. For instance, if the charity provides care for children it may be a teddy bear. Keep the design of the cut-out simple. Attempt to get copies of it donated or at cost. Ask volunteers to cut them out for you. Make way more than will likely be needed so that each employee has a huge stack and doesn't risk running out. Donors are invited to put their name or a message on the cut-out. The paper cut-outs are then taped to a wall or other prominent area in the place of business by a staff member. To reduce damage to the walls, I recommend using scotch tape in tape loops. Keep the campaign going long enough to fill the entire area in which the business is allowing the paper cut-outs to be posted. Provide thank you cards and information about the organization to employees to encourage their support of the campaign in future years.

82. STREET COLLECTING

Asking for donations on the street or sidewalk is a popular way of collecting funds in high-traffic, frequent-stop areas. This type of a fundraiser is easy to organize if volunteers are available to give their time.

First, make collection tins. These can be easily made from used coffee, formula, or protein shake tins. Cut a long, rectangular hole in the plastic top of the tin for donations to go in. Then, print out a sheet of paper that says, "Donations for..." and includes the organization's name, logo, and (in smaller print) phone number, and website. Remove any labels from the tin. Then use rubber cement or a glue stick to glue the paper to the tin. Size appropriately so that the page overlaps and there is only one paper seam. Secure seam with a piece of tape.

Approach business and construction supply companies about donating brightly colored safety vests. Have volunteers wear the vests over an organization t-shirt. This will increase their safety and their ability to be identified as volunteers. Ask them to request donations. If a donation is given, have the volunteer give the donor a card thanking them for their gift that has the organization's name and website on it.

The more volunteers you recruit, the more revenue you will make. However, make sure that you have enough staff members available to collect all the tins at each location.

83. STORE FRONT TABLING

Store front tabling is when your organization has volunteers set up a table in front of a popular business in order to encounter foot traffic. These volunteers ask for donations for the charity. Make sure to look for enthusiastic individuals when recruiting volunteers. To increase volunteers' stamina, provide them with folding chairs, as well as a folding table for materials. I recommend volunteer shifts of two to three people not to exceed three hours in time. The volunteers should wear the charity's shirt and have a collection tin. Permission to table must be given by the business owner before the event. I recommend that you get this permission in writing to ensure that you do not have any issues with the manager the day of the tabling.

To increase donations, volunteers should have brochures available. They should also sell organization merchandise such as t-shirts and bumper stickers. After the event, a board member or staff member of the organization should come by to thank volunteers and collect all of their supplies.

84. FLOWER SALE

Persuade a local or wholesale florist or greenhouse to donate flowers. Keep them in water if they are cut. I have seen this done successfully with paper flowers as well. A small paper flower was $1. They were handmade by volunteers in advance of the event.

Sell them through street collection or store front tabling. Make sure to provide volunteers with large, easy-to-read signs that say, "Carnation, $5, to Support ..." This tells passersby everything they need to know. Make sure the sale price is an amount for which it is easy to make change.

85. CHOCOLATE SALE

You cannot beat the universal popularity of chocolate. There are many chocolate manufacturers that offer fundraising programs where they give 50% of the proceeds of the sale of fundraiser chocolate to the organization at $2 a bar. If an organization uses adult volunteers, this price point and profit margin is too small to be worth your volunteers' time. However, if you are utilizing children as volunteers, these chocolate programs work well. They set an attainable price and a manageable about of money for a child to be responsible for.

In the event that you do not work with a manufacturer's program, I recommend buying chocolate in bulk or at wholesale prices. Add a secondary label to each bar that provides information about the organization that is being supported including its name, logo, website, and phone number. Preserve the ingredients list by keeping the original wrappers on the bars. To increase donations, make wrappers interesting and artistic. Use comedic language on the wrappers and signs. For instance, resell 100 Grand Candy Bars with a sign that says, "Your Donations are Priceless."

Sell $1 chocolate bars for $5. If you find resistance to the price mark-up, tell prospective donors that the chocolate bars are a thank you gift for their donation. Then have volunteers sell the candy in their communities to their friends, family, and neighbors. If possible, have volunteers also sell it through store front tabling.

86. RESTAURANT WORK SHARE

Some restaurants offer work share programs for nonprofit organizations. They provide the organization with a donation in exchange for volunteers working in the restaurant for free. For instance, there is an Italian restaurant that offers unlimited free breadsticks. They will donate to a schools sports team or club if members of that group hand out the free breadsticks to their customers. The amount that is donated depends on how many hours of free work are provided by group members.

Check with a labor attorney before signing up for any of these programs to verify that they are not in violation of any labor laws. Then, make sure that your group members are willing and committed to doing the work before signing the organization up for participation in the program.

87. GIFT CARD SALE

Companies like Great Lakes SCRIP Center (www.glscrip.com) and Fast Track Fundraising (www.fasttrackfundraising.com) offer simple and easy gift card sale programs. Volunteers pre-pay for a set of gift cards. These gift cards were purchased by the participating charity at a dramatically discounted rate, often up to 50% off face value. Volunteers then sell those gift cards at face value. The difference is profit back to the organization.

Most people will purchase a gift card to their favorite restaurant or retailer at face value to support an organization. As a result, this is a very easy sell for volunteers to make.

I have seen these programs be very successful for parents selling on behalf of their child's school. Some schools will even let parents defer some tuition costs by making that money back to the school through gift card sale fundraisers.

88. CHOCOLATE TASTING

A chocolate tasting is a delicious event where attendees get the opportunity to sample many chocolates from multiple chocolatiers. Attendees pay for admission. I recommend a discount for tickets purchased in advance. If this event becomes popular enough, you may be able to charge chocolatiers for the pleasure of being able to give away chocolate at your event through vender tabling fees. However, this requires significant attendance, sales, and press coverage.

At the event, participants move around from table to table trying samples and purchasing goodies from different chocolate vendors. If possible, get a chocolate fountain and fruit donated from a catering company or restaurateur to serve as your event centerpiece. Offer attendees chocolate appropriate beverages such as Champagne, coffee, tea, and water.

89. CHOCOLATE TOUR

On a chocolate tour, a volunteer takes participants from chocolate shop to chocolate shop, tasting a sample at each location. At each site, the tour guide provides interesting and unique information about that specific chocolatier. The tour should start outside one shop and end at another. For this event to work, the tour must be held in an area with at least four chocolatiers within walking distance from one another. This means that large cities are much more likely candidates for the event.

Pre-sell tickets for a discount in advance and also sell them before the tour begins. Contact chocolatiers in advance to get their participation and commitment to give out samples. To prevent any embarrassing incidents on the tour, have your guide call each shop before the tour begins to remind staff members who currently are working on site at the tour. At the end of the tour, give everyone a brochure about the organization and thank them for their support. Tour guides should find a way to distinguish themselves, such as with a flag or sign. This event has no overhead costs, but requires the commitment of one or two chocolate-loving volunteers.

90. Valentines

Selling valentines is a low price point fundraiser. Set your expectations regarding income low. As a result, it works best if the sellers are children or the buyers are buying in bulk. I recommend you take the latter approach and have adults sell valentines to parents they know for their children.

This works well if you are raising funds for the school or religious organization in which children participate. Ask area designers to donate the designs of the valentines and local print shops to print them. Remember that most valentines are given by young children so any images or messaging on them should be appropriate for all ages. Have volunteers tape on mini candies. Once assembled, let the selling begin.

91. Card Sale

Card sales are generally more successful as fundraisers because you can sell them in boxes of 10 to adults for more money. Designs can be donated from local design professionals or students. The more detail on the cards, the higher the price, so consider if volunteers applying embellishments is economically feasible. Get the printing of the cards and envelopes donated.

Use ribbon or card boxes to group cards. Cards that are blank inside, holiday cards, and birthday cards sell best as box sets. No one buys ten Mother's Day cards at a time. Be conscious of the time of year of selling when choosing design themes. Make sure to avoid any themes that are not consistent with the organization's image in the community.

Ask volunteers who are selling the cards to prepare them. This will prevent the organization from being liable if the cards are lost, stolen, or damaged.

92. Gift Wrapping Paper Sale

Sally Foster (www.sallyfoster.com) is the industry leader in gift wrapping paper fundraisers. Their beautiful wrapping paper is often sold for schools and after school programs. 40% of sales goes back to the schools. Other companies also provide gift wrap sale programs, such as Indiana Ribbon (www.giftwrapgifts.com) and Innisbrook (www.innisbrook.com). They may offer a more favorable cut to organizations. I prefer not to utilize corporate fundraising programs that do not provide a comparable percentage of profits to the organization. Ask yourself if giving a corporate partner $6 for each $4 your organization raises is appropriate. If the amount that comes to the organization is incredibly high, it might be worth the cost.

Instead, consider selling hand-painted custom wrapping paper. Have volunteers take preorders from their friends, family, and contacts on an order form. The form should include the purchasers' name, phone number, the number of rolls they would like, and the type of rolls they would like. Use standard pricing, such as $10 per roll.

To make the paper, first get rolls of white postal wrapping paper or bulk paper. This may be donated from a school or mailing supply store. Butcher paper is a fine substitute if it is free. Measure out 5 yards, then cut. If possible, cut with crazy or decorative scissors. Each 5 yard piece will be one roll of paper.

Purchase cleaning sponges that do not have any cleaning chemicals pre-added. Cut them out into shapes for the paper. Each different color of an image will have to be a different sponge. For instance, for Christmas paper, I cut the shape of a candy cane to be dipped in red paint. I cut the shape of a piece of holly leaf to be dipped in green paint. I also cut a little cylinder to be the holly berry to be dipped into red paint. I then made a Christmas tree by cutting a triangle for the tree, a small rectangle for the trunk, and a little star for the top. I then purchased green, red, and yellow acrylic paint. For birthdays, I made presents, which were constructed with a square, a plus sign, and a bow cut out of sponges I purchased in bulk from a hardware store.

Put the paint in small amounts on disposable paper. The sponge should be dipped into the paper so that only one side gets wet with paint. Test the sponge on a scrap sheet of paper before using it on the wrapping paper. If the image works begin randomly painting the image onto the unrolled 5 yards of paper. The sponge will make multiple marks before needing to be re-dipped into the paint. Let dry at least 24 hours. This requires lots of table space, such as that found in a cafeteria. While the finished product is not as a formal as papers sold by fundraising companies, it is special because it is personal and one of a kind.

To make the painting of the paper more fun, have volunteers paint the paper for the individuals they receive orders from. This will add to the customized nature of the paper order. Also, play music in the background so volunteers will have something to listen to besides just themselves working.

Once the paper is completely dry carefully roll it up. Then include an information sheet that lists the type of paper, such as "Birthday Paper," has a "Made By" line, and reads "Sale of this custom wrapping paper supports…" Tie the rolls up with ribbon. You can get gift ribbon in large spools fairly inexpensively. Volunteers deliver the paper and return the money they have raised to the organization.

93. INK CARTRIDGE RECYCLING

A new trend in fundraising is ink cartridge recycling programs. A company, often an office supply firm, donates a set amount to a nonprofit organization per ink cartridge that is turned in. Typically, this is $1 to $2 per cartridge. The company then refills the cartridges and sells them at a profit. The benefit to the organization is the donation and the awareness of the organization that collection tins and boxes provide. I arranged this type of program with Chicago Green Office Company (www.chicagogreenoffice.com) and was able to raise a few hundred dollars annually. The more volunteers collecting cartridges, the more an organization will make.

Collection is the key to success. Hand out tins to individuals at volunteer meetings, organization gatherings, and special events. Make sure any collection tins you make have your mailing address on them. Ask area businesses and schools to send cartridges to the organization. Do not just rely on in-office collecting. Once at least one hundred ink cartridges are collected, arrange for them to be picked up or dropped off with the company. Make sure to count them in advance of the pickup. Increase donations by making this a year-round program.

94. MOBILE PHONE RECYCLING

A mobile phone recycling program works similarly to an ink cartridge recycling program. When approaching office supply stores about an ink cartridge program, ask them if they will recycle phones, too. A surprising number of people have old broken phones around their house that they do not use or need. Increase revenue by adding phones to your collection. Make sure that the collection tins have photos of both an ink cartridge and a phone on them.

95. Private Donations

A private donor is a person who gives to your organization. I have found that most of a nonprofit's donations come from many middle income individuals giving small gifts and a few large private donors giving big ones. Finding a private donor is similar to securing any other donor. They just give more money and may require additional explanation of how it is spent, and/or recognition in your organizational literature.

Cultivating private donor relationships is essential for a nonprofit to be successful. This means finding individuals with disposable income who are committed to the cause, and convincing them to donate.

First, an organization must promote itself in the community. This includes activities such as:

- Write and send press releases at least once a month

- Post activities to online community calendars. These are typically found on every media outlet's webpage and on community groups' pages

- Provide a free e-newsletter monthly and let anyone subscribe. Include in it the organization's accomplishments, activities, and upcoming events

- Hold regular public events such as forums or trainings

- Organize frequent and fun fundraising events

In all of these activities, information about attendees should be retained for future appeals, and information about how to donate should be provided. Once an individual has donated, they should be thanked with a donation receipt. If a person donates $50 or more, consider sending a card in standard mail with a handwritten thank you. This takes time, but really sends a message of genuine appreciation.

Many large private donors will want to remain anonymous. This is because some nonprofit organizations and fundraising companies will look at who has given to similar organizations and then try and bring them over to their cause.

The best indication of future giving is past donations. Remember to ask past donors to give again annually. Do not ask them more than twice per year. No one wants to feel that their entire donation was spent on mailers asking for more money.

96. ANGEL DONOR

An angel donor is a private donor who swoops in to save an organization from mismanagement with a large financial gift. If an organization is running a large financial deficit, its directors may choose to go to local news media and ask for story coverage. Try to get coverage from as many news outlets as possible. This will require swallowing a lot of pride and explaining over and over again how the organization got into this situation, and how future management will be more stable and successful. It is more likely for an organization to obtain an angel donor if it is a beloved community institution, such as an orchestra, theatre, opera, or shelter. If the organization is very lucky, it may get an angel donor to save the day.

97. LOAN FROM A FINANCIAL INSTITUTION

Loans can be tempting for a nonprofit organization. However, obtaining and honoring them is especially hard for an organization that is legally run by a board of volunteers.

The process for approval is similar to that experienced by a business applying for a loan. The smaller the loan, the less paperwork you will need. The organization will need to prove that it has:

- Income sufficient to pay back the loan

- Collateral to back the loan, such as a building or vehicles that it owns

- Professional management that will ensure the future success of the organization

- A history of fiscal responsibility

- A Board of Directors insured against liability

Remember that the financial institution is going to want to know why the organization needs the loan. Not all answers are created equally. If the organization needs the loan to bring a roof up to code, it will be much easier to get the loan than if the loan is needed to cover a budget gap left between income and expenses. Operating costs are nearly impossible to get loaned out from a financial institution. The organization will have to prove that it has future income to cover the deficiency, such as a governmental contract that has not yet paid out. I worked for an organization that was able to get a line of credit with no interest charges from our savings and loan to cover salaries until our governmental check was deposited. They issued this loan simply on the basis of our contract with a municipality.

Getting the loan will be a challenge. Be prepared to provide financial documentation and apply at multiple institutions. If a bank says no, find out why. That answer will help better prepare the organization for the next application.

98. Loan from a Private Individual

A personal loan from a private individual is when an individual gives money to a nonprofit organization from their personal funds with the expectation of that money being paid back. I do not recommend personal loans. While they are easier to obtain than loans from financial institutions, they come with additional risks.

However, if you do receive a personal loan, make sure to sign a notarized contract explaining how much will be given, from whom, when the funds will be received, and the terms for repayment. Remember when signing any document on behalf of an organization to sign with the organization's name and the organization's federal tax identification number. The individual representing the organization should sign their name to a witness line only. Never ever use a director or board member's name or a social security number. Use of personal names and identification transfers legal liability from the organization to the individual.

In my experience, nonprofit organizations do not have a written contract for loans, because it is uncomfortable for a director to approach a board member or donor and ask for their loan to be in writing. While the contact is for the protection of both parties, directors report to boards and donors, and asking them for a written agreement may be perceived as a sign of distrust. I recommend that directors explain the request for a written contact by saying that the documentation is needed for future financial audits. This is not only true, but it involves accounting, an area people rarely question because it is out of their immediate depth of understanding.

Repayment plans should be realistic and manageable for the organization. They should also be clearly expressed in the loan documentation. After I was hired at one nonprofit, I discovered that they owed one of their founders $25,000. Since the organization's annual income up to that point was $27,000, it was unlikely that that loan would ever be paid back. Additionally complicating matters was the fact that there was no loan documentation outside of the debit on the financial balance sheets.

99. PREPAYMENT OF SERVICES

Another form of personal loan is prepayment of services. An example of this is when tuition is paid for a full year, but the student has not yet received the education that was paid for. Having that extra money in the bank makes it easier to meet payroll and other financial demands. However, board members and directors should remember that just because there is a bump in income does not mean there should be a bump in spending. Consider having individuals who pay for multiple years or other distant services in advance sign written agreements as to how much of their money will be repaid if they decide along the way that they no longer want the services.

100. FOUNDATION GRANTS

Nonprofit organizations tend to overestimate the foundational grants they will receive. The fact is that the number and amount of grants available continuously decreases as the number of nonprofit organizations competing for them continues to increase.

One way I have found grants in the past is through Donors Forum (www.donorsforum.org). I attended a free webinar they offered, and at the conclusion of the program, they give attendees one hour of access to their foundation database. From that, I did an hour's worth of searching, exported all the results, and saved them to files. Once the hour of access was over, I begin going through the spreadsheets, reviewing each foundation.

Applying for a foundation grant is time consuming. As a result, organizations should not waste time on grants they are not likely to receive. Read a foundation's giving guidelines closely before applying.

Foundations will want you to prepare a proposal with clear and attainable goals, measurable outcomes, a schedule, and a budget. They will also consider the credentials of directors and other donors. Be prepared to invest considerable time in a proposal. Always have it proofread before submitting it.

101. GOVERNMENTAL GRANTS

Governmental grants are grants issued by the federal, state, or local government. Governmental grants scrutinize the same type of things as foundation grants. As a result, organizational directors should allot themselves plenty of time to prepare documentation and write proposals.

The largest provider of governmental grants is the federal government. In recent years, it has become much easier to find and apply for United States federal governmental grants. Go online to www.grants.gov. This website has a user-friendly search feature that will greatly assist in finding appropriate grants. The website will even send out email updates of grants that meet search criteria.

Speak to local civil servants and elected officials to discover if any local grants exist that might be appropriate for the organization. Each state will have a business office that can direct organizations to their grant programs. Many states have staff members who focus on grant management. Their contact information is a matter of public record. Discuss the organization's mission and see if the state provides any grant funds for the work currently being done or the work the organization could grow into doing.

102. CORPORATE GRANTS

Corporate giving is when a corporation provides a grant to a nonprofit organization. These grants range from very small to large endowments. Corporations advertise their giving programs on their websites. They are usually under the titles "community involvement" or "community giving." Like foundations, corporations provide very specific guidelines for the types of organizations they support. Review these carefully before investing the time in applying. In my experience, asking for a small grant is a great way to establish a relationship with a corporation that can grow in the future.

103. BUSINESS DONATIONS

Many small businesses and franchisees provide smaller donations to organizations in their community. These businesses are often staffed by owner-operators. I have had much greater luck in getting donations from small businesses than from large ones.

A great way to get support is to go door-to-door during a time of day when there is little business, such as early morning for retailers, or midday for gas stations. This method takes a lot of time, so volunteers should be enlisted to help. Bring along organization brochures, a donation form with a tear off receipt, and a copy of your tax exemption letter. Some owners will literally open up the cash register and give you cash or a check on the spot. Others will ask you to leave information and follow up later or simply say no.

When I am looking for business donations, I use chamber of business directories to get a list of all the businesses in the community. Then I go one-by-one contacting them via phone and email. This allows me to reach out to small businesses throughout a large region without having to travel the state for support.

No matter how you reach out to small businesses, remember not to nag, subscribe them to any mailers, or follow up too frequently. One follow up is plenty. If they do give, remember to send them a thank you in writing with a tax donation letter enclosed. I mail businesses thank you cards for gifts over $100, and email all donors tax donation letters regardless of the size of their donation.

104. ANTIQUE SALE

Collect gently used antiques from stakeholders and community members. Then, organize a sale in your building or in donated space. If all the antiques were donated to the sale and all the workers are volunteers, then the sale will provide straight profit.

Have a plan for what to do with goods that aren't sold. I recommend having a specific amount of time that a donor can pick an item up before it will be turned over to a thrift store.

The great thing about antiques is that most people do not know what they are worth, so instead they pay as much as they feel is appropriate. As a result, the price of goods varies greatly. Mark the price of each piece clearly with sharpie-written-on masking tape. Make sure to promote the antique sale:

- In shopping, interior design, and decor publications

- On special event calendars

- In your press releases, newsletters, and on your website

- To interior design professionals and students

- To area antiques dealers

Also, be sure to invite organization stakeholders to the event.

105. ANTIQUE STORE

An antique store operates an antique sale in the same location year round. The key to a successful antique store is to provide the shopper with the type of shopping experience they might get at a high end décor shop. It should not feel like a thrift store or it will only generate thrift store income. The space should be clean and free of dust. The staff should be well-dressed, friendly, and informative. Price tags should be made with professional looking paper tags and string. The market position of the store should not be "charity shop," which brings images of thrift stores to shoppers' minds. Instead, the store's name and atmosphere should send the message, "trendy antique store benefiting charity."

As with other stores, try to find a free or at-cost space. Delivery services are essential for an antique shop. If delivery services cannot be donated, then look for at-cost options. Get bids from every company in the area before choosing a service. Promote the store to the same populations to which you would promote an antique sale.

106. FURNITURE SHOP

A furniture shop may be a good fundraiser if your organization can arrange for free or discounted space, inexpensive or free staffing, and most importantly, can accumulate products from the community to sell for free. To open a furniture store, an organization may need to collect furniture for months to a year and store it until they get a sizable enough inventory. Remember that not every donation is created equal, and items that are significantly damaged or badly stained should not be accepted.

107. FURNITURE RENTAL

Operators of antique stores, or even some high-end thrift stores, may be able to create a side business renting out furniture. Contact all the developers in the area about the shop. Ask them to rent some of the furniture for their showrooms. They may refer the request to a decorator or designer with whom they work. These professionals will select the pieces from the collection to use. Then, the developers will pay to borrow the furniture. Since the furniture was donated, this is an all-profit fundraiser.

Apartment management companies also commonly rent furniture for their display units, but the big get is furnishing corporate apartments. Corporate apartments are apartments similar to long term hotel stays on short term leases. The resident is traveling in the area and as a result, the employer pays for them to be at a corporate apartment. It is nicer and often cheaper than spending three months at a time in a hotel. Corporate apartments need all the comforts of home, and that is where furniture rental comes in.

Rental furniture can also be made available to the general public. In this way, the market for the service is expanded. Individuals new to the area may want to have a few temporary pieces until their own furniture arrives or their designer has completed their work. In the meantime, they pay a monthly rental rate and may even decide they want to purchase the furniture and keep it. With all rentals, I recommend that a credit card is kept on file to charge monthly. This will help with ease of billing.

Offering rent-to-own options is another great way to expand this service and increase income. Just make sure the terms are fair and reasonable. No one wants to think of a community charity as a loan shark.

108. CONSIGNMENT SHOP

A consignment shop is a store where all the goods sold are on loan from the manufacturer. Once they sell, the shop gets 50% of the proceeds and the manufacturer gets 50% of the proceeds. In the area where I live, there are high end gallerias, trendy women's clothing stores, and clothing thrift shops that operate as consignment shops. The product line is up to you. In my opinion, it is a bad idea to combine a thrift store and a consignment shop. It is better to sell new items or high-end gently used goods on consignment.

The great thing about selling goods on consignment is there is no need to purchase inventory. Instead, reach out to area artisans and manufacturers to find great goods to feature in your shop. The better the product for the market, the more the shop will rise in funds. Have a consignment agreement with every vendor in the shop. This agreement should spell out who sets the prices for the goods. It should also waive your responsibility if an item is stolen, lost, or broken.

Like with most shops the largest costs are associated with staff time and space. As a result, try to get retired volunteers to staff the shop as frequently as possible. Also, try to get space donated or at-cost. The more overhead costs are lowered, the more the shop will bring in for the charity.

109. Farmers Market

Organizing a farmers market is easier than you might expect. First, find a space in the community where there is a significant amount of foot traffic. Then, approach the local government about getting the permits necessary for a farmers market. This may mean closing a street or simply renting a park. Park rental is the cheaper and easier option.

Once the space is secured, develop an agreement with a table and tent rental company for free or discounted rates to provide tables and tents for the market all season long. Seasons are typically from Memorial Day to Labor Day. Markets are usually open only on the weekends, with holiday weekends providing an extra day of sales.

Now it is time to secure vendors. Send the table rental form with rate information to anyone who may be interested. This includes:

- Farmers in the region

- Co-ops

- Artisans

- Religious organizations

- Clubs and associations

- Businesses including chamber members

- Nearby manufacturers

Send the form as a pdf via email to everyone with an email address to save money. Provide a discount for nonprofits and vendors who sign up early. All of the organization's income comes from the rental fees on spaces at the market, so make sure that they are all rented out all season long.

110. Farmers Market Stand

Increase your organization's income by having a stand to sell merchandise at the farmers market. If a community already has a farmers market, contact the organizers and ask them to donate space for the charity to use. Then find volunteers to work at the table selling goods and collecting donations. Make sure to hang a banner for your organization at the stand.

111. Cleaning Day

A Cleaning Day fundraiser is organized to have volunteers hire themselves out to friends and family one day per year to clean. The money that they make on Cleaning Day goes to the organization.

Cleaning Day can be renamed to be themed for the charity it supports. For instance, "Detail Detroit for Lake Conservation!" or "Kids Care is Cleaning Cooperstown!"

There are no overhead costs for this fundraiser. Cleaning supplies are provided by the individuals having the cleaning done. Labor is provided by volunteers and clients. Staff simply needs to collect the proceeds.

112. Day of Service

An adaption of Cleaning Day, a Day of Services is when clients and volunteers hire themselves out in the community for miscellaneous work. There are several benefits to the Day of Service over Cleaning Day. These include:

• Most people do not like cleaning, so you will likely get more volunteer participants

• Individuals can hire themselves out for any service and as the market value of the service increases the donations will, too.

• The range of services possible is so great that the event makes for a much more interesting story for the press to cover. They can show anything from plows clearing driveways to a dentist doing a cleaning.

113. CLEANING SERVICE

If you have cleaning staff that are facing hourly cuts due to lack of work, consider hiring them out as a year-round cleaning service. You could use a combination of part-time staff and volunteers to provide a cleaning service with unit prices or hourly rates. To avoid transportation costs, look for customers within walking distance of the organization's facility. The overhead costs of this fundraiser will be staff time and cleaning supplies. Make sure your prices are high enough to warrant the administration of the service.

114. CITIZEN'S ARREST

A Citizen's Arrest is a special event fundraiser where an individual is "locked up" in a public jail or gallows and cannot be released until their fundraising goal is met by their friends and family. The prisoners are volunteers. They send out messages to their friends and family before they are locked up. Some organizations rent "jail houses" which are only big enough for one or two people to stand in at a time. Others have local police departments put their fundraisers literally behind bars.

This type of fundraiser was very popular in the 90s. Personally, I think it is tacky to pretend to be wrongfully imprisoned or waiting to meet a bond amount to be released from jail. I believe that fundraisers should be fun and social, and not be reminiscent of real life criminal situations.

115. SPORTS MEMORABILIA SALE

A sports memorabilia sale is when an organization collects sports stuff from stakeholders. This could be autographed shirts, cards, balls, pictures, uniforms, etc. Once the items are collected, the organization sells each of them. This event is great because the only overhead cost is staff time to organize it.

Promote this event to:

- All stakeholders

- Memorabilia shops in the area. They may want to donate goods to sponsor the event, post the event flier on their wall, and/or attend and purchase goods

- Sports collector clubs

- Sporting goods stores

- Sports associations or clubs

- Gyms

- Sports publications

- Collectors' publications

- Collecting and auctioning clubs and associations

- Auction houses and other places where sporting goods maybe sold

At the sale, make sure to have security and to run credit cards as items are being purchased. Don't forget to write thank you letters to all donors of goods and purchasers for their support.

116. SPORTS MEMORABILIA ONLINE AUCTION

Consider selling the items at an online auction to reach a larger audience. Use a free or inexpensive auction service. Promote the sale to the same audience you would locally, but do so throughout the country. Email potential buyers with the auction info and a link for them to see the auction.

Make sure the auction is long enough to allow for time to promote it but not so long that individuals do not bother bidding. I recommend a week. eBay offers a search tool that will let you see how much similar goods have sold for lately so that you can set a reasonable starting price for the goods.

117. SPORTS MEMORABILIA LIVE AUCTION

The benefit to the sports memorabilia live auction is it may drive up prices past their market value due to competitive bidders. The downside is that unlike online auctions, a person or their representative must be present to do the bidding. This limits attendees to the same individuals who would come to a normal sale.

Hold the auction before a sporting event in proximity to the stadium. This will increase the event's attendance. Be aware that this may also increase the number of individuals who pay immediately, but wish to collect the good after the event.

118. PREGAME SPORTS BOOTH

Set up a booth outside a stadium to sell peanuts or other goods before a sporting event. If an organization is able to consistently get volunteers to work, this will be a great fundraiser for the organization. The only cost will be the goods being sold. Make sure sports officials approve the location of the table before volunteers are scheduled and goods are procured. A letter showing that volunteers are allowed to be there selling should be provided to volunteers just in case any questions are raised.

With a simple banner that says something like, "Tailgate for San Diego's Future" or "I ate peanuts for the women of Peru," an organization will be able to attract consistent foot traffic. If the booth becomes popular enough, an organization can sell shirts at it with catchy sayings like, "I played ball for the Women of Peru."

119. CELEBRITY GRAND SLAM GAME

One fundraiser that is regionally popular on the west coast and in the Midwest is a celebrity grand slam game. It is a celebrity softball game where income is derived from:

- Standard ticket sales to watch the game

- Premium ticket sales to watch the game and attend an after-event reception with the celebrities

- Food and drink sales at the game

- Sale of celebrity signed memorabilia after the game

- Sale of one position on each team

While the potential income is appealing, there are significant overhead costs that must be managed. Staff time organizing the event is high. Because organizing the event takes so much staff time, consider holding the event annually to develop best practices. The venue of the game should be donated. Renting a stadium is out of the budget of most organizations. Celebrities will have to donate their time. Security will need to be provided. Organizations may be able to get this donated by off-duty police officers. Food, drinks, and other goods being sold will need to be procured. With enough planning time, these could be donated or provided at cost.

Getting celebrities to participate will be difficult. However, if they do, the media will cover the event. The organization will receive lots of free press from the media talking about the event before, during, and after it. The organization may even be able to fill a press box and hold a press conference after the event with celebrities being interviewed as to how the game went and why they support the cause.

120. Celebrity Flag Football Game

A celebrity flag football game is similar to a celebrity softball game. Celebrity softball offers better seating and, as a result, higher ticket prices. However, there are many benefits to flag football over softball. These include:

- It can be held anywhere, including a public park, so there are more and less expensive options for venues

- There is a lower chance of someone getting hurt, so it is more likely that celebrities will want to play

• Less equipment to purchase

• Attendees can easily choose to wear red or blue to support the team of their preference

• You are more likely to get attendees from foot traffic in the park

121. COSTUMED CROQUET

Costumed Croquet is a fundraiser where individuals pay to play and watch a croquet game. The organization picks a theme and all attendees dress for it. Popular themes include Victorian, Halloween, vampire, and 1940s croquet. Some towns have Victorian croquet clubs that may be interested in helping organize the fundraiser if Victorian is the theme chosen. When choosing a theme, remember that the event represents the organization. Do not make the theme too obscure or no one will know how to dress for it. Remember that the costumes are just to make the event more fun and get more press.

The game is simple and croquet sets can be purchased online starting around $20 or at a local garage sale. Organize a tournament and sell food. The winner should get a trophy.

122. BAR EVENT

A bar event is a fundraiser in a bar. Most offer some form of entertainment. Money at the door and proceeds from drinks go to the charity. Deals may be brokered with venues to use the space on off nights for free. Do not pay to rent out the bar. It is far too hard to make that money back.

Some bars have private rooms they will let organizations use for free. They will write off the rental on space that was not rented anyways.

Sell tickets in advance and offer a discount for pre-purchase. Remember to make it clear on the ticket sales website that identification will be checked at the door to confirm everyone is 21 and older, and refunds will not be given to individuals who purchased tickets but do not attend or cannot get in due to their age.

123. DRINKING FOR A CAUSE

If an organization does not have the community support to fill a bar, then consider working with a bar on a smaller scale. Have them sell a specialty drink whose sales support your organization. The bartender can create and name it. Offer to print and provide table tops to help promote the sale of the drink. The bars may be willing to also have a menu item benefit the organization. The best way to get their support is to ask them for it.

The benefits to the bar include:

• Opportunity to support a good cause

• Name and address on promotional material including eNewsletter, press release, and website

• Tax deduction

• Opportunity to test a new drink or make a drink with ingredients they already have but have not been selling

• Support of patrons who see drink on menu or on table top and know that the bar is doing good work in the community

Try to get as many bars to participate as possible at the same time. This will increase revenue and media coverage.

124. CONCERT

Holding a concert can be a very lucrative fundraiser. First, you will need to find a free venue. Renting a bar or concert hall is expensive, so look for free or at cost spaces. Public parks or outdoor amphitheaters are easier to get donated.

Find and book bands willing to donate their time in exchange for:

• The opportunity to support a good cause

• Name and address on promotional material including e-newsletter, press release, and website

• Tax deduction

• Opportunity to expand their fan base

• Opportunity to sell goods to attendees at the event

• Free lunch or dinner that you will provide them

Next, sell tickets through a free or low-cost online service. Offer tickets at the door for a mark-up. Procure donated food and drinks to sell at the event. Sell merchandise, including creative t-shirts, at the event, too. Volunteers can help sell goods.

Finally, promote the event! Send email invitations to stakeholders. Then, send out press releases, put it on the organization's website, and post it to online community calendars. Make tear-away fliers and post them around town. Make leaflets to set out in coffee shops. Get media outlets to donate leftover ad space to promote the event.

After the event, send thank you cards and leftover t-shirts to all the event donors who made the event possible. Remember to send enough for each band member.

125. MUSIC FESTIVAL

Planning a music festival is like planning a series of concerts in the park. Simply apply the same model over and over again. To secure the event, the organization will need permits from the city and its political support. Security must be provided. Be careful not to plan the event when there are too many other things happening in the community. Do not forget to rent port-o-potties, including accessible potties.

See if local music schools, instrument shops, or radio stations would be willing to plan and organize the event to benefit the organization. This saves staff and volunteer time.

126. EATING CONTEST

A hotdog, pie, or other eating contest is an event where competitors try to eat as much of one food as possible in a given time. The event is often made more dramatic by having competitors put their hands behind their backs. At this event, competitors pay to compete for a chance at the prize, attendees pay to watch, and general donations are taken at the door.

These types of events are going out of favor with the public because they are seen as gluttonous. I personally would not organize this type of event because I believe having a charity, for instance a homeless shelter, organize any type of an eating contest sends the wrong message of waste and frivolousness in the face of poverty and need. Eating contests are also very dangerous. People have died while competing in them. Most famously, a woman died in a water drinking contest because she drank so much water she had kidney failure.

127. FASTS

Fasts are events where individuals, usually for religious or political reasons, choose not to eat for a specific amount of time. This is often to bring attention to an injustice. I do not recommend organizing a fast to support or promote a cause. Fasting can be dangerous and supporters may be hurt or killed. Additionally, an organization may lose their liability insurance and be subject to lawsuits. I recommend other forms of less dangerous solidarity, such as wearing ribbons of a specific color. While this does not get the same press coverage that a fast would, it also does not have the same potentially catastrophic results.

128. RUBBER DUCK DERBY

A rubber duck derby is a fun nonprofit event where participants "buy" a rubber ducky. Each plastic duck has a number on the bottom so when a person buys a duck for the race, they are marked down as owning that specific number duck. The buyer's name, phone number, and email address are recorded. Then all the ducks are put into the water to race. The first one to the end point wins. The owner of that duck gets a prize. It often includes a specific amount of money.

This type of fundraiser was originally made popular by municipalities who would put the ducks in local creeks or rivers. However, it is much easier to organize in a pool. It also offers additional opportunities for fundraising.

A youth or community organization can sell the ducks and put them at one end of the pool. Then, through the course of a derby party, they will all slowly move around the pool. Eventually, one will hit the other end first and that will be the winner. At the party, the organization can play music and sell food and drinks. Do not sell alcohol by open areas of water, including pools. Remember to have lifeguards on duty monitoring the area.

129. DANCE-A-THON

A dance-a-thon is a charity event where individuals pay to compete and watch. Refreshments are sold. Then, couples dance to music until only one is remaining. That remaining couple wins two trophies and a prize. This event can be held at any gymnasium or community room, and the space for this event can be donated. DJ services will need to be donated from more than one DJ.

Personally I do not recommend this type of fundraiser. Any competition of endurance opens the organization up to liability for a potential hurt participant. Additionally, the overtime costs and burn out of the staff are prohibitive.

130. DANCE-OFF

A dance-off can also be held in almost any donated space. Have a band or DJ donate music and sound for the event. Find volunteer judges. Participants pay to dance. Attendees pay a small amount to watch the event. Refreshments are sold to benefit the organization.

Choose a theme for the event and invite participants and attendees to dress for that theme. The choice of music should support the theme as well. An example would be a 1930s theme, where the band or DJ would play swing music. Change the theme each year to keep it interesting.

This event should be fun and not super competitive, so do not have individuals eliminated from the dance floor. Instead, have the volunteer judges walk around looking at the arm tags of dancers and picking their favorites. Then, the judges should all meet and choose a winner from those who made it onto most or all of their lists. At the end of a couple of hours of dancing, give a trophy and prize to the winning couple.

Hold the event at the same time of year, annually. This will help keep couples and the media coming back for more. In addition to inviting stakeholders and the public, send special invitations to dance clubs, classes, and associations. Also invite retirees and social clubs in the area.

131. SCRATCH-OFF CARDS

This is an incredibly simple fundraiser. Volunteers sell cards which are games of chance. If the person wins, they either get a prize or are entered into a chance for a prize. Scratch-off cards can be sold at specialty shops. Prizes can be donated from local businesses.

I recommend first checking to see if the local government requires any sort of a lottery or gaming licenses for scratch-off cards. I would also have each stakeholder who was selling cards pay for all of them upfront and then collect the money for the charity to pay themselves back. This will guard against the organization being on the hook for lost or damaged cards.

132. PORTRAIT PHOTOGRAPHY

A portrait photography fundraiser is much like other fundraisers where you are selling a service. The keys to success are lots of customers and donated overhead. If an organization is able to get a photographer to take pictures for this fundraiser for free, then it is halfway there!

Next, sell appointments to shoot pictures. There should be various prices depending on the length of the shoot, and if the customer wants images emailed to them, burnt onto a CD, or printed and mailed to them in the future.

This fundraiser works particularly well if for organizations that:

- Have beautiful outdoor landscapes

- Are accessible to families

- Have members who are children

- Are located in a historical or beautiful facility

If an organization does not fall into any of those categories but would like to use this as a fundraiser, then considering holding the shoot at a donated and appealing space. Remember that the key to success is volume. Use volunteers to get families in and out of pictures quickly and back to completing order forms for prints.

133. LIP SYNC CONTEST

A lip sync contest is a fun, easy-to-organize fundraiser, ideal for groups with access to students or a large membership base.

Performers sign up in advance, bring their own music, and dance on a stage while pretending to sing into a microphone. This event should be for all ages, so listen carefully to any music before approving it for the show. Organizers can attract lots of competitors if they promote the event widely. Try to get local radio stations to sponsor it and provide free on air spots for it. They may even be willing to do a free remote broadcast from the event.

Ask local businesses to donate prizes and try to give every competitor something. Then, charge small amounts to watch. Families will come to see the performance of their child and you will make money on their ticket sales. To further increase income, charge for refreshments and merchandise at the event as well.

134. SPAGHETTI DINNER

Spaghetti dinners are fundraisers where you charge attendees for a meal of spaghetti and bread. These events are very popular as fundraisers for organizations that have access to commercial kitchens, such as schools and religious centers. Their popularity comes from the fact that spaghetti is inexpensive and fast to make, but it is filling enough to charge dinner rates.

If the organization does not have access to a large commercial kitchen, find someone who does and will donate the use of it. Find professionals with a background in catering to donate their time to cook at the event. Servers should be volunteers. Remember that every volunteer who is cooking is one less donor buying a meal so try to recruit new event volunteers to help organize everything.

Depending on the formality of the meal and the beverages provided, I've seen these dinners successfully charge from $10 to $25 per person. Know the audience and the price they are willing to pay. Plan background music provided by musicians donating their time and talents.

135. All-You-Can-Eat Spaghetti Dinner

All-you-can-eat spaghetti dinners are similar to the standard dinners. The difference is that you can charge more per plate because attendees can come up for seconds or thirds. A great way to increase revenue and perceived value is by making the dinner all-you-can-eat. That being said, I would warn against holding this event at high schools, colleges, or organizations associated with either. Students tend to have fast metabolisms, and as a result can eat away profit very quickly.

If you are going to do this fundraiser, I recommend providing unlimited garlic bread, too. It is much cheaper and faster to make than spaghetti. You may be able to get baguettes donated by grocery stores or bread manufacturers: day-old bread may be hard for bakers to sell, but it is easy for them to write off on their taxes as a charitable donation. Toast it with garlic and butter and it will be delicious!

136. Pancake Breakfast

A pancake breakfast is another simple and easy fundraiser. It works especially well for organizations with access to groups in the morning or early morning. As a result, religious organizations tend to do very well with this fundraiser.

The ingredients are inexpensive. Commercial size mixes can be purchased cheaply online. Volunteers staff the griddle. Individuals pay about $10 per person and get coffee, tea, or water, and three pancakes. Some events even provide sausage or fruit to attendees. I recommend keeping it simple and making pancakes the only thing that is heated and cooked. It will keep your griddle open for making more pancakes more quickly. Remember to get volunteers to do the cooking and to have the kitchen space donated. Have music, even if it is a stereo, in the background. Use disposable dishes to keep things simple and easy.

137. ALL-YOU-CAN-EAT PANCAKE BREAKFAST

The all-you-can-eat pancake breakfast is a slight adaptation of the standard pancake breakfast fundraiser. Attendees are invited to eat as much as they like for a flat meal fee that is slightly higher, usually about $15. This fundraiser tends to get more attendees then the standard pancake breakfast. Pancakes are cheap to make, so the income is higher, too.

I recommend also providing fruit and fruit juice because it will decrease the amount of pancakes eaten. Depending on the region and time of year, I recommend apples and/or oranges. They tend to be inexpensive and you may even be able to get them donated from a grocer or grocery distributor. I have had lots of luck with grocery distribution companies providing donations of fruit as long as I pick it up from their industrial center.

138. COOKBOOK

Cookbooks are a great fundraiser. The steps are simple. First, compile recipes from stakeholders. The more people you include, the better the cookbook. If possible, collect high-quality digital photos as well. The format of a cookbook recipe is simple: title of food, name of individual who provided it, list of ingredients with amounts, instructions (beginning with any preheating), and ending with the total yield of servings.

Next, organize the recipes into categories such as baking, entrees, salads, and soups. Some cookbooks organize by meal course or region of the world. Consider the recipes you received before committing to an organizational method. Then, create a table of contents and an index to make finding recipes simple. The table of contents should be organized in the order items appear in the book, including chapter names. The index should be in alphabetical order.

Secure a printer. Some organizations may be able to find a company to donate printing and binding services or the markup on the services. Consider the cost compared to working with a professional cookbook publishing company. There are several firms that will publish a cookbook for a charity and charge a per unit fee for the books. Remember that the less money you pay out for the books the more money the organization will make on each unit.

Once you have your cookbooks, you can begin to sell. Setting a unit cost can be tricky. The price should be attainable for the product but still make a reasonable profit. I recommend charging between $15 and $25 per book, depending on the quality and cost of the book's manufacturing. It's hard to justify spending more, even for a good cause, when recipes are abundant and freely available online.

An organization's best bets for customers are those individuals whose recipes appear in the book. They will want a copy of their recipe in print. They may even buy copies for their friends and family. Then, expand the sales to the organization's online shop and to other stakeholders. Most books can be mailed by media mail to save money on shipping costs.

139. Cake in a Jar

Homemade cake mix is a delicious fundraiser. First, collect jars—mason jars work great. Organization stakeholders can collect them, too. One place I have found free jars in the past has been from a fellow sharer on freecycle.org.

After a large collection of jars has been procured and cleaned, select a recipe for the mix. There are many great places to find these online. I enjoy using www.marthastewart.com and www.bhg.com. Determine what batch size fits in each jar, and alter the recipe accordingly.

Get dry ingredients (typically including flour, granulated sugar, baking powder, and salt) from a grocery store. These can often be donated from grocery stores or grocery distributors.

Print small recipe cards that include instructions for baking time and adding the wet ingredients (typically eggs, milk, and vanilla). These should be printed to the size of tags. Labels with the name of the type of cake and the cause can be made on regular printer paper or very simply with address label stickers made by Avery. Free templates are available at avery.com. Ribbon is also needed.

Once all the parts are in place, gather volunteers with hair under hats and gloves on to help fill the jars. Measure the right proportion of each dry ingredient and put them into the jar. Put the lid on tight. Use the ribbon to tie on the tag. This is done by first tying around the neck of the jar and then putting in a knot. Then, attach a tag and tie another knot. A bow can be added if there is sufficient ribbon. Then, stick the sticker that indicates the type of cake onto the top of the jar.

Sell the ready-to-make cakes at bake sales, yard sales, open houses, or at any other event where there is already a table and there are volunteers making sales. Remember that some municipalities have laws that govern the sale and manufacturing of food products.

Depending on how well the jars are decorated, their size, and the purchasing power of customers, pricing can vary. I recommend offering a bulk purchase discount, for instance, pricing jars at $10 each or 3 for $17. This will encourage customers to buy these items as gifts for other people or to stock up for a last minute baking need.

140. CUP OF HOT CHOCOLATE

A Cup of Hot Chocolate is slightly easier to make and sell than the Cake in a Jar. This is because coffee cups are much easier to get donated. Most people have way more coffee cups than they need. Once the cups are collected, mixes are made in simple baggies with ribbon tying the top. Make sure to put a few marshmallows on the top of the mix before sealing it. Hot chocolate is "just add water," so no instructions are needed. These cups of cocoa can be sold for $7 to $13 each, depending on the cleverness of the cup. I recommend selling these in person, because shipping them risks damaging the cups. Also, the shipping costs can be as much as the product price.

141. Cornbread Mix

Recently, a woman made national headlines by selling homemade cornbread mixes to raise money to save her home from foreclosure. Her great success at making over $70,000 on cornbread sales thrust the sale of cornbread mixes into the fundraising plans of many nonprofit professionals and supporters. Her remarkable results were, in large part, due to national media coverage. However, cornbread is a popular item and her copying her model may prove to be a path to success.

She sold her mixes online. They came in a packet and were made at a local church's commercial kitchen space. She sold them with skillets. People purchased them because they believed in what she was doing, and this is the same reason that people would purchase them from a nonprofit. Make sure the packaging is decorative so that the item will make a nice gift. I also recommend selling them in person at events the organization holds.

142. Sugar Cookie Mix

Sugar cookie mixes are great to sell before the winter holidays. Make the dry mix in a bag with a ribbon. Attach instructions, along with a cookie cutter. Cookie cutters can be purchased in bulk from wholesalers online very inexpensively. The packaging should be irresistibly pretty so stakeholders immediately want to buy them for themselves and as holiday gifts.

143. Pizza Crust and Breadstick Mix

Pizza crust mix and breadstick mix are the same mix with different cooking instructions. The preparation of the mix is similar to the Cake in a Jar fundraiser. The difference is that this mix sells well year-round. You can also up-sell this item and charge more by attaching a pizza cutter or jar of crushed red peppers.

144. LEMONADE STAND

Lemonade stands are a classic fundraiser. Lemonade is made by combining water, lemon, and sugar. The more lemon that is added, the more sugar you will need. Include ice on a warm day. Once your lemonade is prepared, have adorable children carefully supervised by their parents sell the lemonade on the corner of an intersection with lots of foot traffic or very slow motor traffic. Lemonade is sold by the glass. All materials can be donated by grocery stores. By setting up stands all over town on the same day or by rotating stands throughout a community, an organization maximizes revenue. I further recommend selling cookies at the same time. This fundraiser is great for children's clubs and associations.

145. HUG STAND

An adult version of the lemonade stand is the hug stand. Adults sell hugs to passersby for $1 to the charity. All that's needed are some signs, a jar for donation collection, and volunteers to do the hugging. Everyone loves a hug and most of us need one from time to time. Why not get a hug and support someone in need? One great cause for this is veteran associations. Retired veterans can wear their uniforms and hold signs that say, "$1 Hugs for the VA."

146. BREAKFAST STAND

Few items have more selling power then donuts, bagels, and coffee. Set up a stand in front of a gas station, grocery store, shopping mall, university hall, or other area with high morning foot traffic. Make sure to have written permission to be there from the property owner. Permits may also apply.

Then, start selling. Sell items that are donated directly from breakfast restaurants, grocery stores, or that volunteers made. Make sure to have coffee in cups to go. Sell items for round amounts of money for ease of making change. If possible, run the stand each Friday morning to maximize traffic and make supporting the cause a habit.

147. Vehicle Donation

Vehicle donations can provide additional cash to an organization. Work with automotive auction firms, used car resellers, and scrap metal lots to create a plan to liquidate any donated vehicles for cash. Review each car as a separate deal, looking for the most money for the organization, or create a simple blanket agreement with one used car dealer. Arrangements will also need to be made for car collection with one or more towing companies.

Then, promote the donation program to the general public as a way to get rid of their old cars. Provide information on the tax benefits of car donation, and market the organization's program to wreckers, salvage yards, dealerships, used car resellers, auction houses, and car rental companies. In some cases, organizations may be able to work out deals where car wreckers pick up donations for free and then take them to the reseller who will be buying them from the organization. This minimizes staff time and maximizes efficiency.

148. Boat or Other Recreational Vehicle Donation

Boats and other recreational vehicle donations work similarly to automotive donations. Organizations simply work out deals to resell the donated goods for cash. The only distinctions are that these types of donations are less frequent and flipping the goods can only be done through sales to recreation stores and scrappers. To increase the number of these type of donations, promote this program at recreation shops and clubs. To expand the number of reselling options, an organization should consider selling goods through online or live auctions in addition to via recreation shops.

149. Billboard Campaign

A little known fact about advertising spaces is that they frequently go unsold in an effort to keep the rental rates high. In the case of billboards this means that owners may keep a previous ad up for many extra months before the space is rented as they look for new firms to rent the space.

This provides a great opportunity to nonprofit organizations and the owners of the billboard. The charity has a forum to promote their message and raise funds. The company benefits because keeping their space utilized keeps their rates high. Their donation means that their sign will have a fresh poster on it, which will also maintain their rates. Furthermore, they will get to support a good cause and take a tax deduction.

A savvy charity will look to obtain billboard donations throughout the communities in which they operate. This may require them to put the name of the billboard company on their advertisement. For instance, "Call 1-234-567-8910" to donate or volunteer for the Eastern Peace Alliance. This message of hope generously brought to you by BigBusinessBillboards.com." Billboard messages should be easy to read, concise, and should include a call to action.

Another hint in creating the billboard content is to use a Google Voice number. Google Voice allows users to create a number with a specific letter or number combination at no charge. It also provides free forwarded calls to an email box and a regular phone number. That way, as the organization changes staff or office space, the calls are still received by the organization and the correct team member.

Some billboard companies also offer the service of printing, posting and/or painting the sign itself. The cost of the printing is generally high, so that should be provided via a donating business. Otherwise, organizations risk spending more in supplies and staff time than the billboard will raise.

150. WALL OR ROOF SIGN

Wall or roof signs are similar to billboard campaigns. These appeals for funds are painted on the wall or roof of a commercial building, typically in an urban area close to a train and/or main thoroughfare route. Getting these spaces donated is more difficult because the messaging is more permanent. In some communities, city permits are needed to get permission to paint advertisements on buildings.

Once an organization has secured a donation of commercial building space, the next step is to acquire skilled painters and outdoor weather resistant paint and supplies. I recommend asking hardware and home supply stores for the weather resistant paint, brushes, tarps, and other supplies. Painting companies may be willing to donate their services. Look for firms that offer mural services. They will be the most appropriate artists for this type of work. If a company cannot be found that will donate their time and talent, then look to art school faculty and gallery managers for referrals to potential artists.

Remember that any painting created will represent the organization. Accordingly, it should be tasteful and simple. Have a preliminary sketch approved by the charity's management and board of directors before painting begins.

151. Skywriting

Few things get the attention of the public more quickly than skywriting. Skywriting typically costs $1,000 plus expenses for up to 30 characters or letters. Even if an organization is lucky enough to get the fee waived, it is rare to find a company that will donate the cost of the fuel. With the limitation of characters, I recommend stating the organization's website. If space remains, a simple call to action should be added. Examples include, "Help Now!", "Give Back," or "Donate Today."

Sky writing can be done year-round. It most effective on a clear day over an area where there is a large crowd gathered, like a football stadium or beach. Stadiums work well because there is an opportunity for additional viewership through media coverage. This means the sky writing will need to be completed in September or October during game season and in a metropolitan area large enough for a professional or college football team.

The advantage of this method of fundraising is the awareness it creates. There are a few potential detractors to this type of campaign, too. First, an organization might be seen to be garish if they are perceived to be spending money on skywriting. Spectators might think, "If they can afford skywriting they don't need my donation." Second, there is no guarantee that the audience will be receptive to the message. An organization is spending money without targeting a specific group of proven donors. Perhaps attendees at Saturday's football game will visit an animal welfare agency's website, or perhaps they are more likely to donate to a battered women's shelter. There is no quantitative data on this matter, so the skywriting expense is a gamble.

152. PLANE BANNER

A plane banner offers a similar opportunity at similar expense as a skywriting campaign. It also mirrors skywriting in having very limited character space with an almost certain expense. The one distinction is that plane banners do not fade and so can appear in the sky as long as the plane is circling.

This is an ostentatious form of fundraising. I would not personally recommend this method unless an organization is raising money for a flight school, air force academy, veterans' group, or other organization somehow affiliated with planes or flight. Otherwise, this display will likely lead to disgust instead of donations.

153. TEAM MEMBER CAMPAIGN

Team member campaigns are fundraising events where organization employees are asked to set personal fundraising goals for the organization, and they then raise the funds through their own efforts and networks. This is very useful in organizations with large staffs. Recommendations for goal setting can be offered but it is best to allow team members to set their own goals.

It is important to make fundraising optional and not mandatory to keep individuals enthusiastic about raising funds. Mandatory programs force team members to work off hours for no pay. This is illegal and unethical.

One great way to encourage participation is to find businesses in the community that will give coupons and gift cards as thank you gifts to the staff. Organizations should publicly and repeatedly thank all fundraisers, with special thanks going to the top fundraiser. I recommend finding businesses to donate items you can provide as prizes to the top 5 fundraisers. Then, advertise those prizes. This will get the funds from employees' trunks and junk drawers into the organization's bank account. Really large organizations may be able to offer more prizes, as well as supplement the donated thank you gifts with purchased gifts.

Remember to set clear guidelines in advance. Organizations with development staffers should not compete for prizes. They should be organizing the effort and not getting credit for grants and organization events that they put together during work hours for the organization as part of their professional duties.

Make sure there is a clear and easy to remember deadline for turning in funds; examples include December 31st or July 4th. The drive should last 1-2 months, and could be held as an annual event. An organization that ends the campaign in the summer can use it as a reason to have a summer holiday party where prizes and awards are given out to participants and top fundraisers.

154. TEXT TO GIVE

One of the most popular ways to raise funds for some of the largest nonprofit organizations in the world is text-to-give campaigns, and they can work wonders for small organizations, too! Giving is made simple and donors rarely notice the small addition to their bill.

There are several companies that can set up text-to-give campaigns for nonprofits. Some to consider include mGive, Mobile Cause, CauseCast, Give to Cell, g8wave, and iLoop Mobile.

These campaigns can be expensive, so make sure that the standard donation amount is at least $10 per text to cover costs. Set-up fees range from $0 for Give by Cell to $1000 for iLoop Mobile. Monthly fees range from $0 for g8wave to mGive's $400 to $1500 per month. In addition, these companies all charge a transaction fee for each donation. These start at $0.35 per donation for mGive and g8wave, up to $.50 for Mobile Cause. Billing is purposefully complex, and programs and offers change constantly. I recommend that organizations create a spreadsheet of costs and estimate costs based on a realistic level of donations. Then, select the best deal. Organizations should reevaluate their provider annually. Do not forget to promote the program through press releases, donated ad space, the organization's website, and the organization's newsletter.

155. VIDEO PUBLIC SERVICE ANNOUNCEMENT

A video public service announcement is one of the most effective methods of raising awareness and funds for a charity. A public service announcement (PSA) is an informative commercial for an organization that airs on television or radio. Video public service announcements can air on websites, television, online television services like hulu.com and fancast.com, clip sites like youtube.com, and on cable and network television stations. Organizations based in college towns or major metropolitan areas may be able to find local production companies or groups that are willing to donate their time and the use of their equipment to produce a video PSA for your organization.

I was lucky enough to find a production company that made a thirty-second PSA for an organization I directed. They got a cameo in the PSA and their logo and link flashed on the screen at the end. This company also became an annual corporate sponsor of the organization. They covered all the costs of filming and production. I was able to get a car and gas donated to drive us around. We received a high quality video that propelled the organization to a new level. We put the PSA onto DVDs and distributed it to all local television stations. We sent the audio to radio stations. We posted it to the organization's home page and to youtube.com. We asked friends and supporters to rate the video to increase its views on youtube.com. We sent press releases and newsletters out to promote it. We received accolades and donations due to the added press coverage.

When creating a video public service announcement, remember to keep it short. Thirty seconds spots will help local network television stations complete their mandatory PSA time while fulfilling their scheduling and advertising commitments. A script should be written, reviewed, and approved in advance to save the film crew time. The copy should include information about the organization and a call to action. The organization's website should appear on the screen for as long as possible. The filming location(s) should be well-scouted in advance. Organizations should give themselves extra time to get to locations, to set up, and to shoot. Remember that these professionals are doing you a favor, so prepare to be accommodating and offer them food and drinks at meal time.

When the film is done and editing is complete, get copies of the final product digitally and on DVD. The digital versions will be easy to email around once they are zipped in consideration of hard drive and email box space. The DVDs will make for a physical reminder of the PSA at local television stations. In additional to area television stations, make sure that public television and public access stations receive a copy as well. If your organization has resources to purchase PSA production services, I highly recommend Big Teeth Productions (www.bigteeth.tv). The higher the quality of the final product, the more places your video will air.

156. Audio Public Service Announcement

The trick with being successful with radio ads is repetition. The more an audience member hears an advertisement, the more likely they are to act on it. Therefore, audio public service announcements should be catchy and timely.

If an organization has already produced a high quality video public service announcement, then they might be able to take the audio from that video and use that as their audio public service announcement. In most cases, the content will need to be adjusted for the medium.

When writing content for the public service announcement (PSA), consider that not everything an organization stands for or believes in would qualify as appropriate material for a public service announcement. Religious and political beliefs are not appropriate content. However, that does not mean that those types of organizations cannot use this activity to raise funds. A religious organization, for instance, could have an audio PSA with the message, "Citizenship makes our community stronger. This winter, check on your elderly neighbors to make sure that they are safe and healthy. A message from [insert religious organization here], more information about this and other ways to help in our community at [insert website here]." It is important to say the website of the organization clearly at least once. If there are any hyphens or other punctuation, audiences will need to hear it a minimum of twice. By making the content of the PSA entertaining without being offensive, an organization increases its airtime.

The total air time should be thirty seconds. If your organization does not have access to audio equipment, then reach out to local colleges or public radio stations to ask for their assistance in recording and editing the public service announcement. If time and resources permit, record several versions that vary in length, such as a 15 second, 30 second, 45 second, and one minute version. While the 30 second version will likely get the most airtime, the others might get used as well.

Once the audio is complete, email copies of it to all area radio stations. If the clip is for a national organization, then use regional volunteers to get the clip to as many radio stations as possible. The more stations that receive it, the greater the chance it will air. I once received a request from a local station for a Spanish version of an audio PSA. A volunteer recorded it for us the same day, and we were able to extend our message to yet another segment of our community. Online radio stations are yet another option for increasing exposure.

157. PODCAST

The new frontier of radio is the podcast. Podcasts are radio that is streamed or downloaded to a phone, mp3 device, or computer. Most successful podcasts are free. Producers make their money by either asking listeners to give donations, such as with the *This American Life* podcast, or by encouraging them to purchase supplementary products, such as books through the Adam Carolla podcast. Informative and philanthropic podcasts are not just the domain of public radio stations. Many other nonprofit organizations can successfully jump into this area with very little overhead. If an organization provides employment services, they can give 10 minutes of career advice each week. If they offer debt counseling, then the podcast can provide personal finances advice. As an avid listener to a wide variety of podcasts, I recommend having two individuals host. This will be especially helpful in maintaining continuity as an organization experiences turnover.

Remember that, as with all promotions I have suggested, the podcast represents the organization. As a result, the content should be consistent with the organization's culture. I've worked for both stuffy and whimsical charities. They could both cover the same topic on a podcast, but I would prefer to listen to the one produced by the whimsical organization because it will likely provide the podcasters with the space to let their banter flow naturally. At least once during a 10 minute show and at least twice on any show longer than 20 minutes, the hosts should plug the organization, state the website, and ask for monetary support.

There are organizations, such as vocolo.org, that offer free classes teaching how to produce a podcast. The equipment is inexpensive and long lasting. There is even free editing software available online on sites such as download.com. Vocolo.org can make recommendations on equipment and software.

158. SYMBOLIC GIFTS

Many people are familiar with an ad campaign that states, "For just a dollar a day..." The success of this campaign is that it asks for a reasonable commitment from donors and promises tangible results. The idea behind this and other symbolic gifts is simple. An organization calculates the cost of providing anything, such as books for a student, and then tells donors that if they give that amount of money they will be providing a child with textbooks.

Calculating the cost of a good or service is simple. First, determine the unit price of the supplies and add shipping. Then, take all organizational administrative costs, including staff and facilities, and divide them by the total number of services provided. For instance, if an organization operates a soup kitchen that provides 10,000 meals to the hungry per year and the food is all donated, the cost of each meal would be the total overhead costs divided by the 10,000 meals. So if costs such as staff, utilities, and facility rental totaled $30,000 annually, then each meal costs $3.00. As a result, the organization could operate a symbolic giving campaign where they said, "For just $3 a day you could provide a meal to a hungry member of our community in need." This seems like a good deal, because it is less than what the average person spends on a typical meal. Donors could commit to gifts and feel they were purchasing an actual thing, because they were allowing the organization to provide that thing to one more person.

159. Symbolic Adoption

A symbolic adoption is when a donor gives a certain amount of money to provide for the care of an individual thing. An example would be an astrological society dedicating stars to individuals who donate $250. Once a person "adopts" the star, they receive a certificate stating the star's location and the new name given to it by the adoptive owner.

There is no expectation of ownership or collection of the good. The adoption is simply a financial guardianship. A better analogy than adoption would be to call the donor a benefactor, but this term is less appealing to donors.

This type of fundraiser is very effective for organizations that support and protect animals and the environment. For instance, a person could adopt a tree for a conservation group and receive an email photo of the tree. A donor could also symbolically adopt an endangered animal. The donor gets a photo of the animal, along with information regarding the protection that the animal rights organization is providing it. This method is surprisingly effective and any animal can have any number of sponsors, as few people can afford all the care that any one exotic animal needs.

160. SYMBOLIC SPONSORSHIP

Similar to the symbolic adoption, the symbolic sponsorship provides financial support to someone or something. This terminology is preferred when the item being financially supported by the donor is of incalculable value, such as a human being or a national treasurer. An organization could not ask donors to give $50 a month to adopt a child because the child already has parents, and the term adopt has a legal definition that does not apply. Instead, an organization can ask donors to sponsor the child for $50 per month and then list specific resources that the organization will give that child and his or her family for the duration of the sponsorship.

Feelings about these programs are mixed. Because of cavernous distances between the cost of living and value of currency in most developed counties compared to developing nations, it is inexpensive for a person to provide monthly assistance to a child or family in need. While the practices of these types of donations are generally seen as a great benefit to the community that the organization is supporting, some individuals feel that the terminology of "sponsorship" is condescending in the context of a child. Instead, many organizations are moving to the term "support."

Sponsors typically receive photos and letters from "sponsored" children. This is to continue the bond that the donor feels with that child so that they will continue to donate. Some organizations even provide a means for sponsors to send gifts to the children.

In the case of symbolic sponsorship of a highly valued inanimate object, such as the London Eye or the Statue of Liberty, letters seem unlikely. However, photos of restoration work and a hand written thank you card go a long way in ensuring the continued financial support of the donor.

161. PRINT BUSINESS DIRECTORY

A business directory is generally a successful fundraiser for chambers of commerce. The organization lists area businesses. It provides a cross index of information based on industry, area, and name for convenient use. Organizations make money on selling enhanced listings with elements like logos and bold print, and by selling ad space. Then, the directories are printed and provided to residents and tourists all over the area. A great place to hand them out is at hotels. I know of a neighborhood chamber of commerce that consistently makes $50,000 per year on their neighborhood business directory. Residents look for it because it includes coupons in the ad section. Tourists look for it because the neighborhood is historic and walkable.

162. ONLINE BUSINESS DIRECTORY

Online business directories provide listings of businesses. They have search functions that allow users to search by name, address or neighborhood, and/or industry. Similar to print directories, online directories make their money by selling ad space and enhanced listings. Thanks to the power of the internet, an online directory can even favor enhanced listings in the search results by listing them on top. I would recommend this type of fundraiser to other niche groups in areas where local online directories do not currently exist.

I was able to very successfully operate an online business directory, localfirstchicago.org. It raised money for the organization and promoted its mission of encouraging community members to support locally-owned, independent businesses. Its online business directory was successful for the following reasons. First, a local design company, Orbit Media Studios (www.orbitmedia.com), built an amazing and widely envied website with grant money and donated time. Second, we provided a niche service that distinguished the directory from other business search engines such as Google. In this case, it was that the directory listed only locally-owned independent businesses. Third, it allowed searchers to search by specific Chicago neighborhoods that might not show up on a more mainstream search. Fourth, it provided free listings to all locally-owned, independent businesses, which meant that the directory was full and functional. Finally, it provided a simple online directory listing application that included a place for the business to indicate if they wanted a free basic listing or a superior purchased listing. This allowed business owners to complete the listing at their convenience, day or night, which was especially helpful for sole proprietorships.

163. PRINTED MEMBER DIRECTORY

Membership directories are a simple fundraiser that provides information about the organization's members. They are indexed and searchable by name and other demographic and geographic information. Funds are raised on printed member directories by selling ad space to area businesses and/or by selling copies to members. Provide clear deadlines for information to be submitted to encourage participation.

164. PRINTED MEMBERSHIP BOOK OR YEARBOOK

A printed membership book or yearbook is a book with members' names, contact information, professional and educational accolades, family information, and a photo. Imagine it's like a much more detailed yearbook for adults and families. This type of fundraiser works great with sororities and fraternities, with professional associations, and with religious groups or associations.

It should be made in a quality high enough to be a keepsake. That means no ads. Income should be made on the book sales alone. There are many companies that provide printing and binding, so shop around and use member contacts to save on overhead and increase fundraising revenue. Include photos. If possible, have memberships submit the photos so that they are flattering and individuals will be more likely to want a copy of the book.

Set the price at a high but attainable level. It will be simple to calculate income potential. If the cost of a unit is $5, then the per unit profit at $25 each is $20. If all 100 individuals listed in the book buy at least one copy then the book profit is $2,000. Give every member an order form and encourage them to buy one copy to display and one copy to keep for future generations.

I recommend using a free online form service like surveymonkey.com to collect members' information. Let them know that what they type is what will appear in the directory. Then, have the completion page instruct members to email their photo to an email address with a very high space limit, such as a gmail.com account. This makes collection of member information and construction of the book easy.

165. Online Membership Directory

Online membership directories serve a different niche then the printed membership directories. Thanks to the advent of free online social networking sites like facebook.com and professional networking sites like linkedin.com, it is a challenge to provide an online membership directory for which an organization can charge. Only organizations specifically targeting business professionals will have success in this endeavor. If an organization chooses to sell access to the directory, then it should be part of an up-sell package that includes other special premium membership features, like access to the association's LinkedIn group.

You will dramatically increase the success of your online membership directory if you provide access to members for free and make your money on the ads sold on the site via an ads service like Google or Amazon. Make sure to get express permission to list a member's personal information and have the site secured through a log in.

166. Pet Auction

A pet auction is a fundraiser where shelter animals that would otherwise be euthanized are instead auctioned off to the highest bidder. This type of fundraiser is typically successful for animal shelters or animal care groups. For organizations that take care of animals every day, the steps are simple. First, carefully groom and dress up the animals. Try to get a local pet shop to donate animal clothes and nice collars. If you are unable to get those, use ribbons.

Then, schedule and promote an auction date at a nice location with a stage or where a stage can be erected. Invite the public and the organization's stakeholders. Put the organization's pre-adoption application online. Then invite attendees to complete it before the event and get pre-approved for adoption. Bring copies with you to the event so that individuals who did not complete the pre-approved application can still bid on pets.

Provide drinks and snacks to attendees. Play music and encourage mingling. Then, let the auction begin! Have the master of ceremonies start with an explanation as to why it is important to support the organization and its work. Then, he or she should explain how the winners will collect their pets after the auction. The auctioneer should describe each pet well, including what type of home would be ideal for it, as a volunteer walks the animal out on stage. Finally, start the bidding!

At the end of the event, volunteers will facilitate meetings between the new owners and pets. Individuals who did not complete the pre-approval application will have to complete the application before the adoption will be complete.

One potential downside to this type of fundraiser is that it does not allow animals to meet owners naturally to see if there is a personality fit. The organization relies on attendees to hear the auctioneer's description of the animal and what home would work best for it, and then classify their own home and purchase a pet. One way that some organizations avoid this challenge is by inviting bidders to the event early to meet the pets. This requires more volunteer time, but may increase the likelihood of a good match.

If space and refreshments are donated for this event, then there are virtually no overhead costs and nearly everything is fundraising profit. The additional benefit is that animal's lives are saved at the same time.

167. PET RENTAL

Pets are expensive. They need space and attention. Ownership is not right for everyone at every point in their life. There has been a boom in recent years of pet rental in major metropolitan areas. A person pays an hourly or daily rate for pet ownership. At the end of the time, or before, the pet can be returned. This is a simple fundraiser for animal shelters and protection groups. It also provides a way for individuals who do not have the right home or lifestyle for a pet to have the opportunity to play with one for an extended period of time.

When choosing a pet to rent, make sure its temperament is right for the job. Pets should also be attractive and well-bred. Animals that are affectionate and outgoing are ideal. When the renter shows up, they are given an introduction to the pet's personality, likes, and dislikes. They're given water and food dishes and a leash they must return. To save time, renters can purchase food at the shelter, too.

Research the organization's market to determine the price point of this service. In many areas, renters pay up to $1,500 per year for rental privileges. Have renters put a credit card on hold with the office or a cash deposit down for the rental. This will help ensure the safe return of the animal.

168. Service Auction

A service auction is a fundraising auction where the items auctioned off are intangible services. If an organization has many supporters but few individuals with the financial backing to give significant donations, ask them to give to a service auction. Many services are very valuable. Auctions can feature services such as carpentry, painting, massage, or a private chef for an evening. Staff members may even want to offer services in the auction.

This auction can be done online or in person. In my experience, service items auction better online when the maximum number of bidders will have an opportunity to see and bid on them. The great thing about this fundraiser is that it incurs limited efforts and expense to the organization, and yet has the potential to raise significant funds.

169. Date Auction

Date auctions were a popular fundraiser of 1980s and 1990s television. The concept is simple: men dress up in suits and are auctioned off as dates for a night to a room full of women. Women are never auctioned for obvious cultural reasons. In contemporary times, the auctioning of men is frowned upon as well.

However, if an organization chooses to have this type of fundraiser, the set-up is similar to that of a pet auction. The auctioneer describes the man and then the audience bids. At the end of the night, the winners schedule dates with the men on which they have bid. Their credit cards are charged and a donation goes to the organization.

170. Restaurant Gift Cards

Restaurant gift cards are a great fundraiser around the winter holidays. The cards are purchased at a discount in bulk from a vender. Then, they are sold by the organization's members or supporters for their face value.

Some companies even offer a three price point model. For instance, the price the organization pays to buy the cards is $10 per card. The price the supporter pays to buy the card is $20. The value of the card when it is used in the restaurant is $30. This provides a financial benefit to everyone in the transaction. Companies with the three price point model include fundraising.com, fastrackfundraising.com, and www.buyforcharity.com.

I highly recommend that organizations have their stakeholders pay for the cards they are reselling or using themselves when they receive the cards. This way, an organization is not out money if a volunteer loses cards. Try not to order more than are needed by asking volunteers to commit to how many they can sell for the organization in advance of ordering them.

171. Renaissance Fair

A Renaissance Fair is a festival where volunteers and often attendees wear renaissance era clothing, speak in an old-fashioned dialect, and engage in period activities. Attendees pay a small fee to enter, and children are typically free. There are stage shows to watch and other organized activities.

Organizations also raise money through booth rental to merchants. Typical items sold include leather goods, jewelry, art work, candles, soaps, costumes and clothing, pottery, wooden goods, furnishings, and toys. Merchants are encouraged to offer product demonstrations and engage visitors.

Another opportunity for revenue at a renaissance fair is to have the organization be the exclusive food seller. Typical food items sold are pig roast, turkey legs, mead beer, corn on the cob, baked potatoes, and bread. Some fairs choose to have guests eat exclusively with their hands. Bring lots of napkins.

Most fairs last for a three day weekend. An organization's first attempt at this event does not have to be that ambitious. Organizing this type of fundraiser requires a significant commitment of volunteers' time and talents. Without a large and supportive volunteer base, organizing this event is not realistic.

172. Historical Fair

Nearly any historical period can be converted into a festival. Few periods have the following that the renaissance fairs can tap into, but any other historical period can generate a themed festival. This includes less positive times in history like colonial times, so choose carefully. I recommend not choosing a period before all citizens received the right to vote.

173. Music Festivals

Musical festivals are outdoor celebrations of live music. Funds are raised primarily through ticket sales. Additional income is generated through merchandise and refreshment sales.

Festivals, fairs, and any other events using public space must be planned well in advance to secure permits. This often means planning a year in advance. When securing a permit, make sure the event date is on a day when there are no other major music festivals in the region.

Use local music experts to select a variety of musical performers that are likely to be popular in the area. Secure their services for as close to free as possible the first year of the festival, since you have no way of guaranteeing that ticket sale revenue will cover expenses. In future years, it will be possible to offer the same groups an increased fee. Consider arranging for sliding scale fees based on advanced ticket sales, if possible.

Arrange for security with the local police department. Rent port-o-potties. Many companies recommend one restroom per 100 attendees and 10% wheelchair accessible restrooms. Some companies charge extra for same day pick up, extra toilet paper, or hand sanitizer, so make sure you receive detailed quotes before you select a vendor.

Tickets should be sold online in advance for a discount and at the door as space allows for a premium. There are several online ticketing services for nonprofits that offer free services, so I recommend shopping around.

Promote, promote, promote! The vast majority of the time and effort that is put into a music festival should be spent on promoting it. This will sell advance tickets. All of a nonprofit's events should be hyped to their stakeholders through invitations, electronic invitations, newsletters, the organization's website, in press releases, and on online community calendars. Musical festivals should also be promoted on music blogs, at instrument shops, at music schools and instructional facilities, and at music venues.

174. CONCERT

If a music festival is too much commitment, build into it by starting with a concert. Find a venue to donate space and musicians to donate their time and talents. Some venues will have sound and lighting equipment available, while others will require that outside venders provide it. School bands and bands looking for exposure are often willing to perform once for free if they are given the opportunity to sell their music and merchandise and given a free meal.

175. CONCERT SERIES

A concert series is a great fundraiser for any cultural group. Book a variety of musical performers at different venues across a metropolitan area. Sell individual venue tickets and offer discounts if purchasers buy series passes to all of the performances. Have a different volunteer act as Master of Ceremonies at each event and introduce the performers and the cause.

Organizing a concert series is exponentially more work than planning just one performance. However, with a series, an organization receives significantly more income, does not strongly affiliate itself with one type of music or demographic group, and gets more mileage for the promoting dollars and time. If an organization is in a dynamic climate where the weather can be unpredictable, I recommend a concert series over a music festival because it is indoors and can be held in the winter months when fewer cultural and social events are available.

176. LECTURES

Lectures are popular fundraisers among private libraries, museums, and private clubs. At a lecture, the organization arranges for a prominent speaker to read an excerpt from a book or give a speech. Then, audience members can ask questions. Finally, the event concludes with time for individual attendees to speak with the lecturer and if applicable, buy and sign books. Income is generated through selling tickets to the lecture. Many groups provide dinner and basic drinks, which dramatically increases the price point of the tickets.

I have attended many of these events, and they provide a great way for community members to meet prominent figures while supporting a nonprofit organization. I have heard national political figures and children's book authors speak. I once heard an anthropologist discuss the historical importance of the color blue in northwestern Africa. The options for an organization vary greatly.

The key to keeping revenue high is finding attendees through local clubs, networking groups, universities, and libraries. The trick to keeping costs low is finding speakers who are willing to waive their speaking fee for the opportunity to speak about something they love for an organization they support. Some organizations are able to win grant funding to underwrite the costs of providing high profile speakers. An example of a foundation that has funded a lecture in the past is the Ploughshares Fund (www.ploughshares.org). Look for organizations that support the cause behind the lecture topic. They will provide strong underwriting leads.

177. LECTURE SERIES

A lecture series is a group of often themed lectures that a nonprofit puts on to raise awareness about an issue or the organization, and to raise funds. An example would be a human rights group planning a series of speakers on various topics relating to human rights. Having the speeches held in a predictable pattern will make it easy for individuals to remember to return and attend again. Income is generated from ticket and refreshment sales. Offer discounts for pre-purchased tickets and series passes to all the lectures.

While a lecture series does take time to plan and promote, it is a great way to share information about a cause while raising funds. The activity is seen as a service to the community by funders and attendees and as a source of income by fundraisers.

178. PANEL DISCUSSION

A panel discussion is an ideal fundraiser for an organization whose mission is to increase the public dialogue or knowledge of a particular issue. Panelists should be carefully chosen to ensure that they are knowledgeable leaders in the field, willing to donate their time, and effective public speakers. Space for the event should be donated. The panelists should sit behind a table on a stage or risers. Income from the event comes from ticket sales and supplemental donations given at the event.

The event begins with a Master of Ceremonies (MC) introducing the cause and the panelists. The MC should then give the audience instructions as to when it is appropriate to ask questions. I recommend that the each speaker speaks and then the floor is opened for questions. This ensures that there is time for each speaker to complete their presentation. The MC is responsible for making sure that each question is on topic and that the event does not run over time. At the end of the event, the MC will once again thank the attendees for coming and the speakers for speaking.

179. ONLINE PANEL DISCUSSION

Thanks to the convenience of the internet, many of us learn, work, date, and communicate online. The medium works wonderfully to provide an international platform for an online panel discussion. If an organization's mission is create cross-cultural dialogue, why not have speakers on the panel who are living around the world? Many speakers who are too expensive for an organization to host in person can be available to them via an online panel discussion.

The technical stuff can be simple or highly sophisticated, depending on what you'd like. Webcams are needed to film the speakers. High resolution cameras can be purchased online from many manufacturers for about $20. An organization can use basic conferencing packages from providers like Go To Webinar (www.gotomeeting.com/fec/webinar) or Tech Soup (www.tech

soup.org). Some organizations may prefer to operate a group call line on services like Skype (www.skype.com). However, not all of those programs make muting the group while someone is speaking possible. Whichever program is chosen should allow a moderator to speak to introduce each presenter and to ask for donations. See if the tech provider will provide a link to the organization's donation site from the webinar window itself.

Presuming the panelists donate their time, the total cost for an online panel discussion should be under $500. Donations are not guaranteed, so attempt to recruit as many attendees as possible. This way, the organization achieves a larger public presence even if it does not bring in a significant amount of money on the day of the online panel.

180. PUBLIC FORUM

A public forum is a fundraiser where an organization secures a location with audience seating and a microphone in the front. Attendance is free. Funds are raised through donations made via donation boxes at the doors. Audience members take turns speaking to the group. A facilitator thanks attendees for coming at the beginning and end of the event and asks for donations to support the organization.

Community groups specific to a small geographic region tend to be the only types of organizations that can successfully hold and make money from a public forum. I do not recommend it for most nonprofit organizations.

181. DEBATE

Organizing a debate is similar to organizing a panel discussion, but there are a couple of key differences. First, in a panel, the speakers frequently agree about most things. In a debate, two people with polarized views about a topic argue for an allotted time and nothing is resolved. Generally speaking, the group that organizes the debate should not have a "side" in the debate. For instance, the groups that host political debates should not be political. It harms the standing of an organization when it is seen to take an extreme view on any topic. Debates tend to get more attendees and press coverage then panel discussions or individual speakers. Controversy breeds conversation. So the trick for an organization is to find a debate topic that is interesting enough to get attendance and speakers that are dynamic enough to maintain the attention of the audience. However, you do not want the controversy be so interesting that it turns people away from the organization or the cause.

Secure free space. Universities are a great venue. Have a speaker introduce the charity and ask for donations. Then introduce the speakers and explain any rules of the debate. Manage the speakers' time and their compliance with the debate's rules. At the end of the debate, ask for donations again and thank everyone for their attendance.

If the speakers are influential enough and the topic is timely enough, an organization may be able to charge for admission and have the event televised. Winners and losers of the debate should not be declared.

182. ONLINE VOTE

An online vote is a great fundraiser for a tech saving organization. First, set up a special voting website that links to the organization's site. It should have a short and easy-to-remember URL. Then, place two typically contradictory things up on the site to vote for. Voters get 1 vote per $1 given. So if someone gives $20, they get 20 votes for their side. The site should track donations and have to column graph showing how high each side has gotten. It should display the progress for website visitors.

The vote and contestants should tie into the organization and its mission. For example, an animal shelter could have a vote "Dogs versus Cats" with photos of a dog and cat from the shelter. A hiking club might use, "Spring versus Fall: which is better?" A parent-teacher association might set up a vote to determine which is better, peanut butter or jelly. The ideas are endless.

Once the website is up and accepting donations, start promoting it to stakeholders and throughout the community via blogs and other online forums. Make sure that the website gets as many hits as possible by encouraging members to make it their homepage for the duration of the vote. Send out a special newsletter to launch the vote, and one to remind individuals to get their last-minute vote in right before the cutoff date. Voting should last at least thirty days, but no more than 3 months. This will allow time for interest to build, but not so much time that complacency develops. If the website becomes very popular, considering selling t-shirts that promote each side on the website, too. This can generate a little extra income and provide a plug for the website.

183. Ring Tone

Selling ring tones can be a challenge, given that most people have access to the technology to freely record their own. However, a very catchy jingle or a special holiday message can be an inexpensive way to bring in a little extra money to an organization. Make the ringtone downloadable through online media stores like iTunes and via the organization's web store. If a celebrity supports or endorses your cause, see if they will be a voice on the ring tone. While the unit price of a ring tone is very low, the cost is much lower. This fundraiser is not a great money-maker, but it does increase the organization's visibility in younger demographic groups.

184. Mobile Device Applications

Some organizations have online services like business or member directories that would be helpful to have available in a user friendly application. With the help of a technology grant or pro bono services, an organization can offer a mobile device application (app) to allow users to conveniently access information or services on the go.

There are two fundraising strategies for apps. First is the pay-per-download system. The organization sells the application to a user through online music and data websites like iTunes and via the organization's web store. Each download costs a specific unit price. The second strategy is to offer the application for free as shareware. Then, ask users to donate if they appreciate the service or want the organization to continue its work. In the second strategy, the organization gains access to many more users that may or may not become future donors. However, the organization may be able to convert those individuals into more long-term supporters by using the app to invite them to fundraising events.

185. SCREENSAVER

Screensavers are those often annoying, animated programs that come onto a computer screen when the screen has been inactive for an extended period of time. They are popular in business environments where individuals do not want passersby to see the computer screen if they have to step away from their desk momentarily.

An organization can use a technology grant or pro bono services to create and sell a screen saver. The content can vary from something entertaining to a bouncing logo. An example might be for an heirloom vegetable cooperative to have the top of the screen read, "Thank you for supporting Veggie Village Co-op," and the animation on the bottom of the screen could be plants growing. Brainstorming with the developer will help create a plan that supports the fundraising model and the organization's vision. The more sophisticated the animation, the more space the screensaver will take on the hard drive and the more resources it will take to develop it.

Once again, there are two ways to monetize the screen saver. First, an organization can sell the screen saver. This seems less than ideal, since nearly all computers have a sleep function which is free, comes on the computer, and performs the same function. Second, the screensaver can be offered as a thank you to donors who give a donation of $25. Then, it can include a humorous thank you message and be a premium for the donation as opposed to a standard purchase.

186. GROCERY STORE SAVINGS CAMPAIGN

A grocery store savings campaign is a fundraising crusade where stakeholders are asked to set aside the funds they save each time they go to the grocery store and give them to the organization. For instance, if a person goes to the grocery store, spends $100, and the bottom of the receipt says, "Today You Saved $5.25," then that person would donate $5.25 to the organization. If this is done on a monthly basis, few people notice the out-of-pocket donation, yet most organizations will greatly benefit from and appreciate the extra $25 per month or $300 annually they receive from participating donors. This is a simple way for people to give without feeling a huge hit to their family budget. I highly recommend this fundraising campaign to organizations with large groups of constituents. It's unique, simple, and continuously engages donors in thinking about the organization.

187. ART FAIR

Art fairs are great way for cultural institutions to showcase art while raising funds. To organize an art fair, secure an easily accessible and free space. Then, find venders such as galleries and arts organizations to rent booths at the fair. Finally, promote the event to organizational stakeholders and throughout the cultural community. This includes sending invitations and leaflets to collectors, museums, curators, university students, and art supply shops.

Income from this event is drawn from booth rental space and from any refreshment sales that occur at the event. I would discourage any group from charging for entrance. The bigger the crowd, the more buyers there will be. The more buyers there are, the more booths will be re-rented.

With all festivals and fairs, but especially with niche groups like artists and art aficionados, it is important to make the event an annual occurrence that happens at about the same time each year. It will dramatically increase traffic to the fair, as well as save staff time.

188. ART SALE

For organizations that are not in the culture business, an art sale may be a more appropriate fundraiser. After hours, the organization's office can be cleaned up and used to display art, or another free space could be utilized. Artists can donate pieces. Alternatively, artists could sell items with half the proceeds going to the artist and the other half to the organization; this is the customary arrangement between artists and galleries. Clients or other community members could make pieces, too.

The organization should provide light refreshments during the sale. Volunteers should welcome guests and offer them information about the organization. Artists should be invited to attend and mingle with potential buyers. The event should be open to the public and highly promoted. Lots of traffic is the key to increasing fundraising revenue and passing along the word about the organization to a maximum number of community members.

189. CULTURAL FESTIVAL

Cultural festivals are a great opportunity for the public to sample a cornucopia of cultural experiences. One of the best festivals I have ever attended showcased music, poetry, dances, and food from across the Middle East. The organization that put on the event had a mission of promoting peace in the region. One of the ways they wanted to do that was through cross-cultural appreciation. As a result, the organization of the festival became both a mission project and a fundraiser. Income came in from sponsorships and booth rentals.

Cultural festivals also work as great fundraisers for trade association and refugee groups. For instance, an international refugee and asylum-seeking group may want to put on a cultural festival that highlights the cultures of the immigrants they are primarily assisting. This would serve to offer those individuals an opportunity to share their culture with the community, as well as to invite members of that ethnic or cultural group to get involved with the charity's efforts. Alternatively, a trade association like the Mexican American Trade Group would want to highlight one culture exclusively.

190. FOOD FESTIVAL

A food festival is exactly what it sounds like—a festival of food! This type of fundraiser is ideal for organizations that promote tourism or the restaurant industry. Some well-known food festivals include the World Food Festival (worldfoodfestival.org), Taste of Chicago (tasteofchicago.us), and the relatively new LA Street Food Festival (lastreetfoodfest.com). Fundraisers can get great ideas and insights from these events' websites.

Organizing a food festival is similar to organizing any other festival. The major distinction is that vendors for the event will be restaurants and chefs. Reach out to them for participation at least one year in advance, and offer them a discounted vendor rate if they commit early to a booth space.

At the festival, organize activities like tastings, cooking classes, and product demonstrations. Recruit volunteers from the ranks of culinary school instructors: they are skilled and not afraid of the spotlight. If bands or DJs offer to play the venue for free, then definitely schedule them. However, music is not a necessity for a food festival.

I recommend making admittance free. If that is not fiscally possible, entry for adults should be inexpensive and offer free entry to children. Income should come from booth sales primarily, if not exclusively.

191. FOOD FIGHT

The 'Tomatina' Tomato Fight is the most famous public food fight in the world. Each year, an average of 30,000 visitors come to Buñol, Spain to throw more than 240,000 pounds of tomatoes at each other. The event brings international attention and a massive infusion of tourism revenue to the small Spanish town. Food fights are fun and a great source of fundraising for municipalities or tourism boards.

The downside to a food fight is obvious. Using food as a toy or for entertainment instead of for nourishment in a world where people die of hunger can be perceived as being insensitive or wasteful. An organization will have to determine if the community will perceive a food fight as an exciting activity or a demonstration of excess.

For organizations that choose to organize a food fight, the key is selecting an appropriate food. Tomatoes are ingenious because they are so messy. The food that is selected should be readily and inexpensively available in the area. It should be soft enough that it does not hurt when someone is hit by it. Ideally, it should be something that is appropriate to use after it is no longer good to eat but before it's completely rotten.

An additional complication in planning a food fight is planning how you will clean the streets and the participants. If the event is held in a park, perhaps everything could be hosed off, as they do in the streets of Buñol. However, the more water that is used for cleaning, the more risk there is of overflowing the sewers, which will not encourage tourism.

192. FILM FESTIVAL

Film festivals are a fun way for arts, cultural, and media groups to explore any topic. A film festival is a fundraiser when a series of films are shown over multiple days. Typically, the festival curators select films from those that have been submitted to the festival. Screenings are promoted through a festival website. Tickets are sold through the festival's website as well.

Renting theaters can be expensive, so instead, have theaters donated or use auditorium halls at colleges and universities. Hotels may be willing to donate screening rooms or equipment in exchange for numerous overnight guests being brought in to their hotel for the screenings. An additional benefit to using university space is that organizations can bring in refreshments to sell. Refreshments dramatically increase revenue.

Ticket prices can be increased if the organization coordinates special events around some of the screenings. Ideas include producer and writer meet and greets, panel discussions, and receptions. These provide a more interesting experience for the attendee and more revenue via higher ticket prices to the organization.

To encourage participation in the festival and media coverage of the festival activities, give trophies away for the best films. Make this a special annual award that filmmakers will be proud to win. Contact area film critics and professors to be judges. If possible, announce the winners at a press conference.

193. INDEPENDENT FILM FESTIVALS

Independent films are movies produced outside of the large traditional movie production companies. Independent films tend to be easier to get approved to screen. It is also much more likely to get an independent film's director or cast to participate in screening activities, like receptions or panel discussions.

Most major metropolitan areas already have an independent film festival. A search of the top 100 independent film festivals in the United States found that the majority of the established festivals are held in the spring and early summer. Perhaps this indicates space in the landscape for a fall independent film festival. Boston has an independent film festival in April (www.iffboston.org); LA Film Fest is in June (www.lafilmfest.com); and Nashville's is in April (www.nashvillefilmfestival.org). An online search over an organization's area can let organizers know when other regional festivals are so that scheduling conflicts can be avoided.

Organizations can further distinguish their festival by showing specific types of films related to their cause. For instance, a women's rights organization can show a series of independent films by women in cinema. Alternatively, a peace group could screen inspirational films about great icons of the peace movement. This type of specialized film series helps forward the cause of an organization in a way that encourages a diverse audience that the organization may not otherwise have been able to reach.

194. INTERNATIONAL FILM FESTIVAL

A very popular type of film festival is the international film festival. International film festivals may be even more common that independent film festivals. These festivals are a good fundraiser for organizations that promote travel or business with a specific country. They are also appropriate for groups that promote cross-cultural dialogue, immigrant and asylum services, or other international or multicultural work.

The films are harder to select than for other film festivals, and organizations are less likely to have the director or cast available for events. However, they offer an opportunity for creating community dialogue, so it is well worth the time investment for an organization willing to make the event a success.

Remember when promoting the festival to promote it to community and cultural clubs and associations throughout the region. For example, if an organization is screening several French films, invitations and leaflets should be sent to French language schools, French teachers, French American Associations, and French restaurants. Additionally, information and invitations should be sent to groups from regions where French is commonly spoken, including Belgium, Canada, and many African nations.

195. PETTING ZOO

A petting zoo fundraiser is a fundraiser where an organization, typically an animal conservation group or shelter, raises money by charging visitors to see, pet, and sometimes even feed the animals. Before taking the animals out of the shelter, double-check the organization's liability insurance to confirm that it covers animals and employees in and out of the facility.

Typical petting zoo animals include miniature horses, horses, cows, goats, sheep, royal dainties or other small pigs, cats, dogs, bunnies, chickens, and turtles. If an organization has these animals on site, then this might be a reasonable fundraiser.

The key to getting individuals to pay to attend the petting zoo is to take the animals to a place where people normally do not get to see them, such as an elementary school in a metropolitan area. Contact area public, charter, and private elementary schools. They might be willing to pay for the petting zoo to be offered for their children to experience for free. Then, organizations will not have to charge for attendance or spend time and money on promoting the petting zoo.

Expenses are primarily transportation, staff time, and fencing. Income comes from ticket prices for entry, pet food sold to attendees to feed the animals, and concessions sold to attendees for their own enjoyment.

196. EXOTIC PETTING ZOO

For those organizations based in areas where farm animals are too common to solicit an entry fee, an exotic petting zoo might be more successful. Exotic petting zoo fundraisers might be appropriate for exotic animal sanctuaries. They operate similarly to standard petting zoos, with the distinction being that animals are not native to the area in which the petting zoo is held. Typically, these are animals native to other continents.

Exotic petting zoos are so thrilling to the general public that an animal preserve may be able to open the petting zoo at its facility on a routine basis and charge for admission. This saves on transportation and wear and tear on fence and caging equipment.

While petting and feeding the animals is likely unsafe, the thrill of seeing them can be great, especially for children. Promote the exotic petting zoo to schools, too, as a destination for a field trip. Give vehicle outposts, tourism boards, and hotels brochures about the petting zoo to hand out. Let attendees know that the petting zoo supports the larger conservation efforts of the organization.

197. Exotic Animal Show

An exotic animal show is a theatrical performance where trained zoologists or biologists perform live stunts with animals in front of a live audience. For exotic animal preserves, this is an opportunity to generate a consistent form of income to offset their conservation expenses. Admission charges vary wildly depending on geographic area, the types of animals in the show, and the publicity given to the show.

Promoting the exotic animal show will be similar to the exotic animal petting zoo. Some of the most famous exotic animal shows include stunts like a person wrestling an alligator. However, this type of feat-of-daring based show reflects poorly on the conservation group and inhibits the organization's ability to promote the show as an educational experience for school children and families. An example of a very successful exotic animal show that is educational and entertaining would be Walt Disney World Animal Kingdom's Bird Show. The animals fly and run around and make noises. The human performers make jokes and reward the birds for help with the punch lines. While Walt Disney World is certainly not a not-for-profit organization, it has a successful exotic animal show model that can certainly be repeated.

198. Circus

Circuses have attracted both public criticism and popularity in recent years. Circuses receive the criticisms that they do not treat animals well and that it is not natural for wild or exotic animals to be doing dances or performing other stunts. The increase in their popularity has come from the expansion of the Cirque du Soleil and children's circus groups. Very few not-for-profit organizations make a good fit for a circus fundraiser. Gymnastics groups and children's circus clubs are nearly all of the types of groups that can successfully organize and raise money from a circus.

Remember that when performers are children, there is a high probability of improvisational acting and accidents. Parents should be present and participate in the planning of the show. Funds raised from this type of fundraiser come exclusively from ticket sales, so keep overhead low by using donated space to hold the event.

Promote the event to neighborhood and senior groups, area associations, and arts and children's clubs.

199. DANCE PERFORMANCE

Dance performances are an entertaining way to raise money for art and culture groups. An organization that provides support to Native Americans may choose to organize a dance performance to raise funds. Special event grants may be available to organizations that can show funders that the dance performance forwards their mission of promoting the culture of the group or the type of dance.

Income is brought in through admission charges, refreshment sales, and merchandise. Free locations are readily available through universities, parks and library facilities, and civic groups.

Event promotion should include civic groups, cultural and arts clubs, dance clubs, dance instructors or schools, area activity groups, and associations specific to the type of dance or dancers.

200. CELEBRITY DANCE PERFORMANCE

Celebrity dance performances expand the audience of a normal dance show to the general public. If an organization is lucky enough to have a large group of celebrity supporters or performers, then turning a dance performance into a celebrity dance performance is a great idea. Remember that the more press coverage the event gets, the more interested celebrities will be in participating.

Underwrite costs with corporate sponsorships and make money on ticket sales. Charge different ticket prices based on seat locations. Sell VIP passes that allow premium ticket holders who pay a top ticket price to attend a reception for the celebrities after the performance.

201. CELEBRITY DANCE-OFF

With the popularity of shows like *Dancing with the Stars*, dance competitions have grown in stature. A celebrity dance-off is an ideal fundraiser for a dance company, but it will work well for any organization that has the connections to celebrities to make it happen. By adding the element of competition to a celebrity dance performance, an organization dramatically increases the public's interest in the event.

Consider when selecting a venue that income from the event is finite and comes from ticket sales, and refreshment and merchandise sales. Free spaces are ideal, but capacity is important, too. See if a venue will provide the space for free in exchange for corporate sponsorship of the event.

Judges should be knowledgeable and colorful. Start the search at dance schools. A minimum of three judges should vote on the performance. Winners should be awarded a trophy at the end of the event. The Master of Ceremonies should give out the trophies. He or she should also do a post-dance interview with the winners and ask them why they support the organization.

202. TELETHON

A telethon is one the most well-known forms of fundraising. Telethons are fundraisers where donors call into a special line to donate and a phone bank of volunteers take their credit card information. Some telethons, like the Jerry Lewis Telethon (www.mdausa.org) and the Public Broadcasting System Telethon (www.pbs.org), are broadcast on television and feature celebrity pitchmen and phone bank volunteers.

Not all telethons need to be televised. I volunteered on a telethon that was on closed circuit TV around a college campus. Volunteers were instructed to bring their phone books and whenever they weren't receiving a call to call out and ask their family and friends to pledge. The volunteers were rotated out hourly to maximize the number of outgoing calls to receive pledges.

Telethons work well for any organization with mass appeal and the ability to process credit card donations. Many telethons last twenty-four hours; however, the twelve hours during the day are likely the most effective time to operate. Phone banks can be set up simply through free or inexpensive call forwarding services. Volunteers can receive calls on their personal mobile phones during the telethon and then when they finish their shift, the forwarding can be stopped. This dramatically reduces overhead for the organization and increases the results of the fundraiser. It also makes it possible for individuals to access their contacts lists and make outgoing solicitation calls.

203. WEB-A-THON

Another alternative is to stream the telethon over the internet, making it a web-a-thon. Internet streams are simple and inexpensive. They add an international reach to a standard telethon. They also eliminate costs almost completely. A camera can easily be borrowed or donated and hooked up to a laptop. This also allows donors to give via the website, as well as by calling in. Viewers can see the campaign's progress towards its goals and dialogue with the master of ceremonies.

Organizations that could benefit from a web-a-thon include any groups that are technically proficient or who have access to a technically proficient volunteer. The more interactive and engaging the site is, the more likely it will be linked to other sites and forwarded around. This will increase donations and awareness about the cause.

204. TEXT-A-THON

A text-a-thon is a fundraiser where volunteers text their friends, family, and colleagues and ask them to give to a cause by texting. Each person receives a thank you message that asks them to text their network of contacts and encourages them to give too. It serves as a modern version of the old-fashioned chain letter. The cost to the organization is minimal and the potential gain is great. This fundraiser works well with all organizations, but is ideal for organizations that have a large support base of individuals ages 50 and under.

205. KRISPY KREME DONUTS

Krispy Kreme donuts are a large retail and wholesale manufacturer of donuts. They are a popular brand and, as a result, an easy item to sell for a fundraiser. Krispy Kreme provides up-to-date information regarding their fundraising program, including forms on their website (www.krispykreme.com/fundraising).

If fundraisers live in an area where there are numerous Krispy Kreme retail locations, then I recommending selling certificates for donuts instead of the donuts themselves. The certificates are easier to carry around, and there is no temptation for the seller to sample the goods.

If fundraisers live in areas where the Krispy Kreme retail locations are scarce, then I recommend selling the donuts themselves. The smell of the warm sugary treats will make them practically sell themselves. The fact that proceeds from the sales go to a good cause will further incentivize donors to purchase them.

Remember when comparing and selecting a corporate fundraising partner to carefully consider the following questions:

1. Does this corporation represent the values of our organization?

2. Would our affiliation with this organization negatively affect our current donor relationships?

3. Is our organization getting a fair percentage of the proceeds of the sale of these goods or services?

4. Will these goods be easy for our fundraisers to sell? Or in other words, do these goods have a value to the consumer at their current price point?

These questions will help guide fundraisers in selecting the most appropriate corporate partner.

206. DOOR-TO-DOOR SOLICITATION

Door-to-door solicitation is when a fundraiser goes house-to-house and door-to-door asking for donations. Not all neighborhoods or municipalities allow door to door solicitation. Check with the community for approval first.

This form of fundraising requires a significant time investment on the part of fundraisers for very low results. Few potential donors will give money to a stranger at their door. Many people do not feel comfortable even answering the door to strangers. Accordingly, I would discourage this form of fundraising.

207. DOOR-TO-DOOR FLIER DISTRIBUTION

Door-to-door flier distribution is when fundraisers go house-to-house posting door hangers or leaving leaflets. The information left describes the charity and its mission. It includes a donation slip to send in and information about how to donate online.

Historically, this form of fundraising has been popular among religious organizations. However, I would discourage this form of fundraising. It requires significant fundraiser time and resources. The materials often become litter, and donations are rarely made.

208. BUSINESS DOOR-TO-BUSINESS DOOR SOLICITATION

In business door-to-business door solicitation, fundraisers go from business to business asking for financial contributions. This form of fundraising is more effective than going door-to-door in a residential area. Fundraisers will need to bring informational materials about the organization, donation receipts, and copies of the organization's tax-exempt documentation. This form of fundraising is very time intensive so I recommend utilizing passionate, outgoing, and energetic volunteers.

209. Credit Cards

Charity credit cards are cards whose use provides funds to the affiliated charity. Some examples are branded with the organization they benefit. Instead of offering cash back to consumers or other promotional incentives, charity cards give funds to a 501(c)3 nonprofit organization. Branded cards include Bank of America's American Heart Association card and Chase's World Wildlife Fund cards. Other charity credit cards allow users to donate to the organization of their choice. Some cause cards offer an initial donation upon approval of the credit card. This typically ranges from $10 to $50.

Two cards that I would recommend considering are the One-Cause Visa Card and the Target REDcard. OneCause Visa (www.onecause.com/onecause_visa) allows users to donate to any school or cause. The card donates 1% and $20 when the first purchase is made. The Target REDcard (www.target.com) can be set up to support any school. It gives 1% at Target and 0.5% on other purchases.

210. License Plates

License plates are a fundraiser coordinated through the state's department of motor vehicles. License plate programs are organized on a state-by-state basis, so details vary. In most cases, individuals purchase a license plate at a premium rate. The extra money goes to the designated charity. The plates include the charity's logo or symbol and the website.

To see if an organization can be added to a state's charity license plate program, contact the department directly. Be prepared to provide evidence of 501(c)3 status and complete paperwork.

Many different types of organizations have successfully operated license plate campaigns. The key to ensuring income is encouraging stakeholders to participate by reminding them repeatedly about the program. Use newsletters, websites, press releases, and other free forums to continuously plug the program. The more license plates that are in use, the more people will know about the program and participate. In this way, the program can escalate its own success.

211. COMMERCIALLY-PRODUCED COUPON BOOK

Commercially-produced coupon books are books made by third party vendors and sold by nonprofits to raise funds for the organization. Coupon book companies make different versions for different communities. In each, they print discounts and coupons from local businesses and provide an index for easy searching. One of the most popular commercially-produced coupon books is the Entertainment Book (www.entertainment.com/fundraising/). It is available in over 150 cities in the United States and Canada. This book contains coupons for groceries, retail, entertainment, services, and travel. Special features of this book include additional savings via their website, with login information provided in the purchased book. A charity's profit depends on the quantity of books purchased from Entertainment and the number of those sold. Generally speaking, approximately 50% of income goes to the organization. Entertainment reports that in a 2009 consumer study, they found that the average book contains $15,700 in savings and that the average consumer saves $170 and uses 30 coupons each year.

212. ORGANIZATION-PRODUCED COUPON BOOK

An organization-produced coupon book is a discount book created by an individual charity for their community. For an organization to produce a coupon book, it needs to invest staff time and funds to cover printing and distribution expenses.

Organization-produced coupon books have the potential to earn a cause significantly more funds then a commercially-produced book. Consider the following situation. A commercially-produced book sells for $40 per book. $10 of that goes to the organization and $30 of it goes to the producer. When an organization produces the book, the unit cost is typically much lower, around $5 per book, and the book sells for a little less, typically $30 per unit. This thereby increases the profit per unit for the organization from $10 for the commercially-produced book to $25 for the organization-produced book. If the organization sells 100 copies, then the commercial book would make the organization $1,000, while the organization-produced book would have made $2,500.

Another benefit created in the production of the books is that when an organization reaches out to local business owners about participating in the program, they begin to build a relationship that can be expanded in the future. Furthermore, a coupon book with the organization's name on the cover and every page will encourage purchasers to support the cause in the future in more direct ways.

As a result of these benefits to the organization, I recommend organizations make their own coupon books if they have access to design volunteers or staff with layout and production skills. Make sure that each business that advertises in the book signs a contract with the organization to honor the coupon until the expiration date of the book, typically one calendar year.

213. Campbell's Soup Labels

Campbell's Soup labels have long been a fundraiser for educational groups, especially elementary schools. Up-to-date information about their program can be found online (www.labelsforeducation.com). Schools can sign up to participate via the program's website.

Participation in the fundraiser follows these simple steps:

1. Collect universal product codes (UPCs) and beverage caps from participating products. A list of acceptable products is online.

2. Give the UPC labels and caps to the school's coordinator.

3. The school's coordinator redeems the points for educational resources from Campbell's merchandise catalog, available via their program's website.

214. Box Tops for Education

General Mills provides a program to support schools through purchases, too. The program is called Box Tops for Education. Up-to-date information about the program is available on the program website (www.boxtops4education.com). This program works very similarly to Campbell's Soup labels. Fundraisers review the list of participating products and save the proofs of purchase and box tops, which are collected at the school. The school then uses their box top points to purchase school supplies via the program's website. This program is very popular. They boast on their website that it has given over $320,000,000 to schools—a remarkable feat. The sheer scale and popularity of the program mandates that schools participate. I recommend that the program is coordinated via the school's Parent Teacher Association (PTA). This will help encourage wide participation.

215. MAGAZINE SUBSCRIPTION SALES

Magazine subscription sales have historically been a popular way for organizations to raise funds. However, over the last decade, numerous stories of employee mistreatment at magazine sales companies have called into question the legitimacy of claims that they are affiliated with a nonprofit organization. As a result, a backlash against door-to-door magazine sales has occurred. The impact of this on legitimate nonprofit magazine fundraising is that the market of potential donors is much smaller. Due to this and the overall shrinking of the popularity of magazine subscriptions, I would discourage nonprofits from engaging in magazine subscription sales as fundraisers. However, if your organization does choose to participate, double-check the authenticity of any company's business dealings by using the Better Business Bureau (bbb.org) and the area's Attorney General.

216. T-SHIRT SALES

T-shirt fundraisers are sales of t-shirts to raise money for the organization. When coordinating a t-shirt fundraiser, think first about what the content of the shirt should be. Consider whether a humorous or mission-focused statement would be appropriate. The organization's logo or art might sell well. The content should vary depending on the nature of the organization and the target market for the shirt.

The t-shirt style should depend on climate, the time of year, and popular regional styles. Once the style is selected, get price quotes from numerous vendors. If the organization has an environmental mission, it might be appropriate to only get quotes for organic shirts.

If the organization focuses on trade, quotes for shirts made in-country or fair trade shirts might be the only appropriate ones to consider. A deal may be struck if the organization is willing to put the manufacturer's logo on the back of the shirt as a sponsor. To make an expensive design more reasonably priced, have it printed in fewer colors or in grayscale on a colored t-shirt. In general, the rule is that the more standardized and the larger the order, the lower the unit price. I have placed shirt orders where the cost to us was less than $3 per shirt; in another case, I was able to get a small number of shirts free.

Once shirts have been designed and produced, it is time to sell them. Shirts should be sold through as many channels as can consistently be managed. This can include the organization's web store, at events, through volunteers who put down a deposit, at supporting businesses and retailers, and via tabling.

217. POLO SHIRT SALES

Similar to t-shirt fundraisers, polo shirt fundraisers bring in money based on the number of shirts that are purchased. However, organizations can charge more for polo shirts. Another advantage to polo shirts is that, because they are generally embroidered with the organization's emblem, customers have an expectation that it may take longer for them to receive the shirts. As a result, I have successfully operated programs where a local embroiderer does not buy the materials or make the shirt until the order and money are received from the customer. This prevents the organization from having the liability of purchasing a large number of shirts which may or may not sell. In this way, the organization works as the middleman receiving a donation. This fundraiser is also valuable because the shirts further promote the cause through community members wearing the organization's logo.

218. T-SHIRT DESIGN CONTEST

A great way to increase the interest in a t-shirt fundraiser is to ask community members to submit designs for the shirt. One shirt that represents the organization well is selected to be the winner and is

APRIL R. JERVIS, MBA

used in the production of the shirts. In addition to the recognition, an award or trophy can be given. This is especially meaningful if the organization is an arts group.

A major criticism of design contests is always voiced by the professional design community: that the organization is getting work done for free. While this is true, in the realm of a not-for-profit it may be seen more as a donation of time and talent.

219. ONE-BUYS-TWO PROGRAM

A one-buys-two program is a fundraising technique where an organization sells one item for the costs of two of those goods. Then, it gives the second good to a needy person. One of the most famous and successful users of this fundraising method is One Laptop per Child (www. laptop.org). The price of the laptop to the users is twice the typical cost in order to cover the additional laptop that is being donated. Donors are invited to simply buy a laptop to give if they do not want or need one for themselves. This program can work well for greatly divergent organizations. It works best if the group is able to leverage press coverage to stimulate donations.

220. CORPORATE ONE-BUYS-TWO PROGRAM

A corporate one-buys-two program is a fundraiser where a corporation will donate a second good to a needy person, sometimes via a nonprofit intermediary, if a consumer buys one of the products for themselves. The individual products are priced to cover the expense of the second. The most famous of these campaigns is Toms Shoe Company (www.toms.com/our-movement). Toms uses giving partners in developing counties to distribute a pair of new shoes to children. This service is paid for via the pair that a person purchases in the first world.

Programs like this are a great way to get individuals to expand their ability to give and for nonprofit organizations to passively raise funds. To partner with a for-profit company, begin by contacting the manufacturers of the products the organization distributes. If that fails, go to the wholesale and retail sellers.

221. CONFERENCE

Conferences are meetings of people with a mutual concern. A well-promoted conference provides the public with an increased awareness of a cause. A well-managed conference provides many opportunities for income. Attendees pay a fee to participate. Venders pay fees to have booths. Corporate sponsors provide donations to cover marketing and promotional expenses. Foundational underwriters cover expenses such as food and hotel accommodations.

Conferences should be informative. They should include inspirational speakers and panel discussions. An agenda should be created and publicized in advance, and it should allow attendees to learn about and discuss various issues of importance to them. Attendees should be given handouts and copies of presentations given at the conference. If possible, attendees should earn continuing education credits or professional certifications for attending specific educational programming.

Conferences should have a culminating event such as an open forum, formal dinner, or open networking event. Whatever the event is, it should leave conference attendees wanting more and eager to attend again. At the end of each conference, attendees should be given save-the-date information for the next year's conference, including the city and dates it will be held. Conferences are typically scheduled over weekends to maximize the number of individuals that can attend. Holiday weekends make for more expensive hotel rooms, so they should be avoided.

222. ONLINE CONFERENCE

If membership is scattered worldwide and there are not enough funds or interest to swing an in-person conference, then consider holding an online conference. Online conferences serve as virtual meeting places for members and supporters. They can provide the same educational and credential opportunities as in-person conferences, but with less hassle, travel, and overhead.

To organize an online conference, start by identifying speakers, panelists, and forum topics. The better the content, the more the organization can charge for attendance. Then, create an agenda and use it to promote the conference. Raise funds through attendance charges. When someone purchases a conference pass, they should receive a username and password that allows them to access all the online activities of the group. Materials like presentations can be sent to participants via email.

When scheduling a conference, consider if attendees will be participating as part of their salaried job or if this will be for personal development. If the organization hosting the online conference is a business association or union, then it might be appropriate to hold it during business hours during the week. If the organization assists families with issues like adoption or other personal matters, then the conference should be held on a weekend to allow attendees to participate without taking time off work.

223. WEBINAR

Webinars are mini online conferences. They are internet-based seminars. Many nonprofit organizations raise funds through webinars. Decide in which area your organization can offer expertise, and award continuing education credits in it. If no topics are appropriate, then hold webinars for the purpose of professional or personal development of clients, customers, staff, or other nonprofit professionals. For instance, a homeless shelter might offer webinars for the general public on how to manage personal finances and a household budget, or a career counseling organization might hold classes on professional development, covering how to prepare for a job interview or how to re-enter the work force after an extended absence.

I recommend providing attendees of each webinar with a certificate of competition. This can be used by professionals as a credit on the curriculum vitae (CV) or to excuse themselves for work from the period of time when they were in the webinar. They might be used toward continuing education credits or professional certifications too.

Price the webinars at a competitive price. Online conference services may be donated, but organizations will still have to pay for staff time promoting and facilitating the conference. This cost and a margin for income should be calculated in the webinar's price. Also consider bulk pricing. For instance, a first-time homebuyer class may be divided into smaller topics so that individuals can choose to attend just one class on something like credit reports. Alternatively, they can purchase a six seminar series for a discount and get a first-time homebuyer certification upon completion of all classes.

224. Convention

Conventions are similar to conferences, but they are social and not educational in nature. Attendees may attend some classes, but they primarily come to participate in fun activities and share in their hobbies with others. Conventions are often referred to, in slang, as "cons." Some of the most famous conventions are science fiction conventions. Examples of well-known conventions include Keycon (www.keycon.org) and Comic Con (www.comic-con.org). Trade associations typically organize conventions to spur trade, but they also raise funds for themselves. An illustration of this would be the National Retail Federation's (www.nrf.com) annual convention. Organizations like the American Psychological Association have conventions, too. For any cause, membership associations and specialty groups are great convention hosts. They can pull together a group of vendors and attendees with a shared interest.

Income from conventions comes from individual attendance, corporate sponsorship, and vender booth rental. Conventions should be planned at least a year in advance to provide plenty of time to promote and organize the event.

When planning a convention, first consider the audience. Then ask, "What activities would motivate attendance at this convention for my audience?" Answers are as diverse as conventions, and include networking, sales, building friendships, meeting famous authors or personalities, discussing issues of interest, maintaining industry contacts, and learning.

225. Online Conventions

Online conventions are conventions that meet via the internet. Online conventions generally cannot charge the high price for admission tickets that in-person conventions do. They also generally get fewer attendees because conventions are social, and online conventions allow for less personal interaction. One of the most attended online conventions is the Online International Virtual Assistant

Convention (www.oivac.com). Online conventions have a much greater chance of success if they are targeting individuals who are used to working or playing online.

226. DISCOUNT CARDS

Discount cards are a popular fundraiser among groups with adult members. The concept is simple. Fundraisers sell cards that offer consumers a discount on future purchases. The fundraisers receive the income or a portion of it from the purchaser. The companies that provided the discounts receive revenue when items are purchased in the future by consumers.

Many companies offer discount cards to nonprofit organizations as fundraisers. With most of these programs, the cost per unit goes down as the number ordered goes up. Easy Fundraising Cards (www.easyfundraisingcards.com) offers a 50% margin and up on card sales. Other companies offer competitive cards as well, including Fast Track Fundraisings Card, whose profit margin begins at 60% and goes up from there (http://www.fasttrackfundraising.com/ discount-card-fundraiser.php).

Once a partnership company is selected, an organization should estimate the number of cards it could commit to selling. Then the organization should sell those cards to volunteer fundraisers at their face value. Individual fundraisers should sell the cards and give the proceeds to the organization. Some organizations are able to ask fundraisers to purchase the card directly from them for full value, or to sell the cards themselves to the public and avoid coordinating volunteers.

227. LOLLIPOPS

Lollipops are a delicious and fast fundraiser. While the profit margin and charge per unit is lower than for other fundraising products, the market is large because the price point is low. In other words, while organizations make less money on this than selling a more valuable good, it much easier to sell a high volume of the product because people are comfortable making a low dollar impulse purchase.

Organizations can purchase large quantities of lollipops from buying clubs, wholesalers, or fundraising programs. Remember that the cheaper the product's purchase price, the larger the profit margin. Generally, the cost to the organization is approximately 45 cents per unit and the sales price to the consumer is approximately $1 per unit. This offers a 55 cent per unit profit. As a result, an organization must sell many, many units to raise significant funds.

228. BRACELETS

Fundraising bracelets became wildly popular with the explosion of the Live Strong foundation's wristband (http://www.storelaf.org/wristbands.html). Like other goods sold for fundraising purposes, the margin between the unit and resale prices determines the profit available to the organization on a per unit basis. The added benefit of a fundraising bracelet is that it can raise awareness about a cause.

229. ONLINE PETITION

Online petitions can show support for a cause and help identify future donors. In other words, they can promote the cause and help raise the funding to support it. Petitions can be made via online services or on an organization's website. The benefit to hosting the petition on the organization's website is that the organization can instantly further engage a participant in other activities, including awareness efforts, volunteering, and donating. One popular site for posting online petitions is Change (www.change.org). Third party sites retain signatures, but do not always provide email addresses to organizations, so consider various providers before selecting a location for the online petition.

230. SUBLET

Many organizations have office or meeting space that they do not use on nights, weekends, or during the holidays. All of these times provide an opportunity for a sublet tenant to use the space and pay rent to the organization. Sublets can lower an organization's overhead by hundreds of dollars per month. In some cases, organizations are able to find tenants that cover all their overhead costs. Do not forget to double-check the rental contract before pursuing a tenant. If the organization owns the space, then it may need a special business license to rent the space when it is not in use.

Organizations may be able to secure their own tenant(s). This can be done through online postings on real estate and specialty sites. It can also be accomplished through word of mouth and by contacting after school programs and camps. If organizations are unable to find a reasonable tenant, then commercial realtors can be enlisted to assist. In addition to showing the space to prospective tenants, commercial realtors can provide professional advice and sample contracts to assist in the transaction.

231. PAYPAL

PayPal is a common online payment processor. It accepts funds from bank accounts, cards, and other forms of payment. Organizations have been leveraging PayPal to receive charitable donations from donors unable to give by the traditional check in mail method. In addition to setting up an account directly with PayPal, organizations may want to work with companies that have special additional services for nonprofits, including donation tracking, like Chipin (www.chipin.com). PayPal and support programs offer an additional path to receive donations and are well worth consideration by any organization.

232. ONLINE EVENT TRACKING

Online fundraising event tracking and support services can dramatically increase donations. There are numerous companies that offer these services. They include online donation forms, event information, donation trackers such as thermometers, result tracking, social media interaction, and goal information. Some companies that provide this valuable service include Stay Classy (www.stay classy.org), Just Giving (www.justgiving.com), Razoo (www.razoo.com), Convio (www.convio

.com) and What Gives (whatgives.com). I have used Donor Drive, a service of Global Cloud (http://www.globalcloud.net/?page= donordrive-npo-fundraising), and it was helpful in increasing donations and managing and analyzing donor and participant data.

233. POKER NIGHT

Poker Nights can be a social form of fundraising appropriate to some nonprofit organizations, depending on the organization's goals and culture. Some religious groups believe that poker or gambling of any kind should be avoided. For those groups and their members, a poker event would not be appropriate. The house sells chips and the poker night event makes money when the "house" or dealer wins. Poker Night events frequently sell food and drinks to supplement income. Most municipalities require a special gambling event license to operate a legal poker event. Security is also advised when organizations hold events that receive donations through the loss of funds from donors. Make sure to have experienced poker dealers and poker house rules readily available and signed by each participant before play begins.

234. PARKING SPACE RENTAL

If the organization's parking lot has access to more spaces than it uses, then renting out parking spaces may be an option. The value of parking spaces in some downtown metropolitan areas is very high, often hundreds of dollars per month. With month-to-month or year-long leases, administration responsibilities will be at a minimum. A couple of hundred dollars per month per space can make dramatic differences to an organization's overall budget. For this fundraising activity, the market for spaces determines which organizations will benefit from it.

235. TEMPORARY TATTOOS

Temporary tattoos are inexpensive to provide and can temporarily represent a person's support of a cause. At fundraising events, offer a spray or paint-on temporary tattoo to increase donations. The price an organization can charge for the tattoo depends on how long the tattoo lasts and how much effort is put into applying it. Prices tend to range from $5 for a very simple one color transfer to $500 for a sophisticated and long-lasting hand-painted one. Organizations, especially those affiliated with Indian cultures, may also choose to sell henna tattoos.

236. SLED-A-THON

A sled-a-thon is a fundraising event where children get pledges for the number of times they can sled down a hill on the day of the event. Then during the sled-a-thon children sled and track their times down the hill. After the event, donors give their pledges based on the number of times the child they sponsored went down the hill.

Sled-a-thons are a great way to get children excited about a cause. The activity is so entertaining for kids that it can instill a lifelong love of philanthropy. Many causes can successfully operate a sled-a-thon. Some of the best matches for this fundraiser include children's groups.

Set a date at a public park. Some require permits or rental fees. Print out pledge sheets and organization information, such as brochures or leaflets. Then send the children out with their guardians to get those pledges!

Before the event, have the organization's liability insurance provider print a special event insurance certificate. With any event there is a possibly of accidents, but when children are involved, the probability increases exponentially. Ask parents to attend the sled-a-thon to supervise and to help their children track the number of times they went down the hill. It will be important to have as many adults present as children to help avoid accidents and to monitor the children.

237. PIGGY BANK WITH A PURPOSE

Another fundraiser that is great for children and adults is the Piggy Bank with a Purpose. Each participant purchases or makes a piggy bank. Once they are filled with change they are turned in to the organization for the cause.

Some groups find it inspires success and frequent refills to have an annual kickoff event where participants come together to make their own special piggy banks out of used jars. With a sharpie marker and a little pink felt, any jar can look like a convincing piggy bank. Organizations may want to print out logo stickers with their address, number, and website to stick on all the pigs.

This fundraiser works great for all sort of organizations, but especially for groups that have physical locations that make turning in the change convenient. The more locations an organization has, the more community members will drop off their change.

238. Scavenging

Scavenging is using a metal detector to search for treasures. Organizations like beach front preservation groups have successfully used scavenging days to collect treasurers that can be sold to raise funds for the organization. With the example of a conservation group, there is the added advantage of holding an activity that gets supporters to come out and enjoy the environment.

You can use scavenging to find change, jewelry, and other hidden treasures. Participants should sign an agreement that anything found on the day of the event is given over to the organization. To eliminate the temptation of pocketing goods, collectors should bring up the things they find as they go or put them into special organization bags if fundraisers are very spread out. Participants can bring their own metal detectors or borrow ones from the organization for the day.

239. Career Fair

Career fairs are fundraising events where job candidates meet with prospective employers. These are great fundraisers for university or college groups, career and professional development groups, and veterans' organizations. Income from career fairs can be generated from booth space rental, admission charges, and refreshments. However, I recommend that admission is free to attendees. This will encourage a crowd and drive up the costs of booth space rental. Find a venue that can be donated, such as a school gymnasium or community room. Hold the event on a weekend to expand attendance from just the unemployed to include the underemployed, as well.

When promoting this event, remember to reach out to universities, colleges, career centers, college clubs or groups, high schools, unemployment offices, and veterans' organizations. This should be done in addition to the promotional efforts taken in the community as a whole and with stakeholders. Marketing efforts can include emailing information out. Remember that printing a flier is not necessary for holding a successful event.

240. ROADSIDE SALES

In some areas, roadside sales might be successful. While tabling in front of a grocery store is nice, not all regions have grocery stores that will allow tabling or solicitation efforts on their property. An alternative is setting up a stand or sale on the roadside. This typically requires a permit from the local municipality. Lots of signs and volunteers are needed to attract the attention of motorists. Be mindful of traffic, as accidents between automobiles and pedestrians can be fatal.

241. SEAT CUSHIONS FOR SPORTS EVENTS

Selling seat cushions with the organization's logo and/or name for sporting events can offer a significant profit margin and easy in-stadium sales. Cushions cost between $4 and $20 per unit, depending on the number ordered, the size of the cushion, and the colors in the cushion. The best place to sell the cushions is at the entry during sporting events that have particularly uncomfortable seats, such as metal football stadium benches. Many companies sell stadium seat cushions including Promo Peddler (www.promopeddler.com/ stadium_seat_cushions), Branders (www.branders.com), and Global Sources (www.globalsources.com). Making the cushions the home team's colors will increase sales. Placement in the stadium is the key to maximizing profits, so work with the facilities management to find and secure the ideal location for maximum traffic.

242. Toy Drive

Toy drives are collection campaigns. They typically go into full swing during the winter holiday season. The most famous toy drive is the Marine Corp's Toys for Tots (www.toysfortots.org). Organizing a drive can be done through community collection boxes and/or by asking community organizers to collect toys at their homes and then turn in large quantities.

Many organizations can benefit from toy drives. Charities like homeless and domestic violence shelters or unemployment support services can utilize toy drives to provide holiday gifts to their members.

I recommend networking with area clubs and associations to see if their members will participate. If the organization has specific clients for which it is trying to provide presents, then assign each child a number and provide donors with the number, age, and gender of the child. The donors will put the child's numbers on the wrapped gifts to make it easy to match gift givers up with the intended recipient. This will help donors in purchasing age-appropriate gifts. Some organizations include lists. However, I have found that children do not have realistic expectations on their lists and frequently ask for items that exceed the financial spending cap set by the organization.

243. Secret Santa

Some postal service offices set out area letters to Santa and invite customers to pick up one, fulfill the request, and sent the presents to the return address. This is an especially meaningful gesture when the letters are from addressees living in government housing.

Some charities have successfully taken over this role in their communities. Inviting community members in to pick up letters to Santa offers an opportunity for them to support the organization. Engaging a community member in the season of generosity is the best time to solicit all types of support, including volunteering.

244. SCHOOL SUPPLY DRIVE

Not every family can afford school supplies for their child. Other families can afford to donate supplies to a less fortunate child. As a result, a school supply drive can help an educational or other community organization provide school supplies to needy families. Some organizations expand their drive to include collecting new school clothes, shoes, and backpacks. These goods can be turned in at collection boxes or at area elementary schools. This is a great service to provide in a community with public schools that cannot afford to provide school supplies to all children who cannot afford them.

245. COAT AND HAT DRIVE

Similar to other drives, a coat and hat drive collects goods for the needy. Many religious organizations collect coats and hats when the weather turns cold in the area. This drive is especially popular among churches at Christmas time. Used and new coats and hats are very valuable to the needy in regions where it gets below zero in the winter. The collection and distribution of winter coats, gloves, and boots is an important service that an organization can provide the community at little or no cost to the organization.

246. CANNED FOOD DRIVE

Canned food drives are collections of nonperishable food items. This includes canned goods, jars of sauces, dry noodles, and some unrefrigerated beverages. Organizations such as food pantries and soup kitchens rely on food donations throughout the year to operate. However, need and donations increase at the end of the year. Canned food drives can supplement the cupboards of organizations and needy community members.

Canned food drives can be organized with collections at schools, libraries, religious centers, and other community locations. Prizes should be given to encourage mass donation of cans. For example, each grade at a school could compete to see which can bring in the most cans. The winning grade could get an award like a pizza party or an extra-long recess. Whatever the prize is, get it approved in advance of the event and make sure it is free to the organization.

247. Service Dinner

Thanks to national media coverage, service dinners have recently become popular. Service dinners are free meals for members of the military to thank them for their service. These are commonly scheduled on holidays like Thanksgiving and Christmas for service members who do not have family in the area with which to celebrate.

The dinner is free to the member of the military and their family. Food is donated by community businesses and families. The dinner consists of home-cooked food provided at the home of a host family. Service dinners range from one to two people to very large groups. These can be further monetized by asking companies to sponsor them.

248. Refugee Family Sponsorship

For organizations that support asylum and refugee seekers, having a native family sponsor a refugee family provides many forms of support. First and most obviously, it provides financial support to the organization. Secondly, it helps an immigrant family build friendships and a support system in their new country of residence. For immigrants coming from dramatically different cultures, this valuable connection will help make the transition less stressful. It will also better prepare individuals for the challenges of finding employment.

Helping a community member become self-sufficient can be expensive. Interfaith Refugee and Immigration Ministries (http://irim.org/sponsor.htm) estimates that it spends between $5,000 and $8,000 to help a family of four become established in a new home. This entire amount is rarely provided by one sponsor because it is a significant commitment to be made by a community member. Instead, many organizations set up co-sponsorships where families donate a portion of the expenses, such as $1,000.

249. FAMILY SPONSORSHIP

In many communities there are families who need support services due to expended periods of unemployment. Family sponsorships can be arranged by domestic violence or homeless shelters, transitional living facilities, and religious or other aid groups. Sponsor families may provide food, used furniture and clothes, or donations. They typically do not provide the companionship that is part of refugee family sponsorships. Sponsorships should be arranged through a professional fundraiser or development officer at the organization to maintain the anonymity, safety, and security of participants.

250. SCARF AND MITTENS SALE

Hand-knit scarves and mittens are a valuable and useful gift. For a needy person, they mean warmth. For the rest of us, they mean comfort. Retirees are a great source of donated time and talents. Work the retiree groups to get scarves and mittens donated. Charities may be able to get yarn donated from local craft and fabric shops. Sell the scarves and mittens with a tag letting the purchaser know that they supported the cause. This helps purchasers feel good twice! Prices range from $30 to $500 for a set, depending on the material and brand name. Consider what price point will sell all of the scarf and mitten sets and then get selling!

251. COOKIE DOUGH FUNDRAISER

Cookie dough fundraisers are fundraisers coordinated through a cookie dough manufacturer and sold by fundraisers. Profit margins vary and typically range from 35% to 50%. Successful cookie dough fundraisers have volunteer fundraisers and not staff doing the selling.

Partnering with a well-liked cookie brand will make sales much easier. Several popular brands offer cookie dough fundraising programs including Otis Spunkmeyer (www.spunkmeyer.com) and Fat Boy Cookie Dough (www.fatboyscookiedough.com/fundraising).

252. Gift Wrapping

Gift wrapping can be a tiresome chore. Imagine if an exhausted shopper found volunteers eager to wrap gifts for a donation to a cause? Many retailers will be delighted to have volunteers providing gift wrapping at their stores. It provides an extra service for their customers without the staffing costs.

I have organized gift wrapping for two different causes at a national bookstore chain. The company provided the wrapping paper and other supplies. In one case, we received few donations because the cashiers where simultaneously collecting for another cause. In the second fundraiser, we received few donations because several of our volunteers did not show up to do the wrapping. If I were to organize another gift wrapping fundraiser, I would do several things differently. First, I would have the retailer agree to only collect for our cause that day. Second, I would triple schedule volunteers and confirm the morning of the wrap. Finally, I would charge for the wrapping. The majority of individuals who got goods wrapped did not donate to the cause, even when asked. If we had a minimum donation requirement, at least we would have received something for our volunteers' time and efforts. Advantages to this fundraiser include expanding awareness of the organization and helping get volunteers involved with the cause.

253. Santa

Charging for children and adults to tell their wishes to Santa might be frowned upon by the local scrooge, but it is as easy way to raise funds for a children's charity. If an organization does not have direct access to a volunteer Santa, then reach out to a Santa association like The Amalgamated Order of Real Bearded Santas (www.aorbs inc.com) to find one. To silence the Grinches in the group, make sure that the charity and its mission are well advertised at the event.

254. Christmas Village

For the more ambitious organization, constructing an entire Christmas Village complete with Santa and Elves will allow for an increase in the entry charge and in attendance. This will help distinguish the event from other opportunities to meet Santa. Materials should be donated and then reused each year. This will help keep the cost of the event at a manageable level. The more Christmas Village actors who donate their time, the more money the event will be able to raise. Churches may organize a Christmas Village complete with a manager scene that is narrated by an angel. Hold the event annually to make it a family tradition.

255. CHRISTMAS LIGHT TOUR

Organizations like neighborhood associations can organize a Christmas light tour that takes participants through private neighborhoods or parks to see elaborate Christmas light displays. Admission prices can vary based on the length of the tour, decorations, and the electrical expense to put on the tour. Tour dates typically run from the day after Thanksgiving until the day after Christmas, depending on the dates of the Orthodox Christmas and its influence on local traditions. If participants are willing to cover the electrical expenses themselves, then this fundraiser maybe a financial winner for the right organization. However, many consumers are now environmentally conscious, so an event that consumes a lot of energy may not be well attended.

256. WIND TURBINES

Wind mills and wind turbines are relatively inexpensive to make in comparison to their selling price. For environmental organizations, being a designated retailer of wind turbines forwards the organization's mission while providing a source of income.

There are many companies that carry a wide range of wind turbine and mill products. An organization should speak to as many as possible before choosing the right business to partner with. Remember that any corporate partner an organization has affects the perception of the organization in the community. Some companies include: Home Wind (www.homewind.net/homewindturbines.aspx), Helix Wind (www.helixwind.com), Bergey Wind Power (www.bergey.com), Southwest Wind Power (www.windenergy.com), and Windmax Green Energy (www.greenpower4less.com). The more expensive the individual unit, the fewer of them the organization will sell, and the higher profit will be for the organization on each unit. Ask the vendor to donate and install a free turbine for the organization after the organization sells the first unit. This will defer the organization's energy costs and serve as a long term charitable donation and capital improvement.

257. HAYRIDE

Hayrides are a popular fall activity. The concept is simple. A hayride consists of an open air wagon or trailer being pulled by a tractor. People ride with hay in the back of the trailer. The ride typically goes through the woods or on other trails. Charities can raise funds with hayrides by charging for admission, and by selling items like hotdogs and marshmallows for attendees to roast over a campfire. While this event is not a huge money maker, it is helpful for outdoor organizations because it identifies individuals who enjoy the outdoors and fosters a relationship with them and the organization.

258. HAUNTED HAYRIDE

Haunted hayrides are activities for around Halloween. They take the traditional hayride and add actors and/or animation to the trip. The idea is to make it a little scarier. Haunted hayrides can charge more for rides then standard hayrides. They are generally appropriate fundraisers for social organization or organizations whose target market is individuals ages 15 to 25.

259. HAUNTED HOUSE

Haunted houses take the scares indoors. These guided tours through a house offer scares that are generally surprise-based. Haunted houses are often not safe for small children, pregnant women, the elderly, or anyone with a heart condition. Consult with an attorney and post an appropriate disclaimer.

The level of sophistication of a haunted house and how many actors are in it will guide the amount the organization can charge for admission. The more volunteers participating, the larger the profit margin for the organization. Finding free space makes a massive difference in the success of this fundraiser, so plan ahead and contact the owners of empty office space or other buildings.

260. JUDGMENT HOUSE OR HELL HOUSE

Judgment houses, also known as hell houses, are religious-themed haunted houses where each room shows a sin. Generally, these fundraisers are organized by more fundamentalist or evangelical sects of Protestant Christianity as a method of spiritual conversion and fundraising. Some religious groups have raised funds by selling kits. Kits to help an organization put one of these events are available online (www.judgementhouse.org). Supporters of these houses feel that they provide an effective form of religious conversion for many participants.

Judgment houses have been under increased scrutiny for promoting religious intolerance and homophobia. They focus on one particular religious belief system and suggest that those who do not believe as they do will burn in hell for all eternity. This is quite a heavy judgment to put on a person who may have a different religious tradition. Personally, I would discourage this type of fundraiser because I feel that the images, such as the scenes of rape, are too violent and not suitable for minors. Themes like rape and murder should not be used for entertainment or to generate profit.

261. LITTLE CAESARS PIZZA KIT FUNDRAISING PROGRAM

Many local pizza companies have fundraising programs that are worth investigating. One national program is the Little Caesars Pizza Kit Fundraising. The fundraiser is simple. Volunteers sell Little Caesars Pizza Kits (www.pizzakit.com). The profit margin is between $5 and $7 per kit sold. As a result, this fundraiser is most appropriate when children are the sellers.

262. Fundraising Consultant

For organizations with no development staff, hiring a fundraising consultant can make all the difference. If an organization is in search a fundraising professional, a great place to start is the Association of Fundraising Professionals (www.afpnet.org). They provide great advice about hiring a professional consultant. They also have a freely available online consultant and resource guide that shows areas of expertise for many different fundraising consultancy companies (http://consultants.afpnet.org/listing/).

When considering a fundraising consultant, I recommend asking yourself:

- Will this partnership be long or short term?

- What realistic expectations do I have for this consultant?

- Do I feel comfortable having this person or company represent my organization in the community?

- What percentage of our philanthropic income am I comfortable spending on fundraising efforts?

- Do I have the time to support efforts led by consultants?

Consultants range in areas of experience and interest, so perform a thorough interview before signing a contact with the company you will hire.

263. African American Cards and Gifts

For organization that either primarily serve or represent the African American community, selling cards and gifts themed to that community will likely provide an increase in fundraising income.

There are several companies that focus on this demographic group and offer fundraising programs. African American Expressions is a card and gift manufacturer (www.black-gifts.com/ fundraising.html). They use catalogues and an online store to sell their goods. Fundraisers purchase goods at a discount and sell them at their normal market price. MSB Gifts offers a 40% profit on all goods sold to nonprofit organizations as part of their fundraising program (www.msbgifts.com/Fundraiser_ep_27.html). They sell gifts like calendars, book marks, and organizers. Carole Joy Creations sells cards for all occasions, with fundraising profits ranging from 30% to 45% (www.carolejoy.com/fund.html). Shades of Color manufactures calendars, figurines, cards, and magnets and offers nonprofit fundraising partners 40% to 50% profit (www.shadescalendars.com).

264. BATTERY SALES

Battery sales are one the most bizarre fundraisers I have seen yet! Organizations sell batteries to make a profit for the organization. Consumers are reluctant to buy batteries from strangers outside of businesses because they do not know if they will maintain a charge. Additionally, as many consumers move toward rechargeable batteries, they need to buy new batteries much less often and so are very likely to not need or want batteries when they are offered to them by an organization. That being said, that are organizations that have successfully operated battery sales by focusing on having their members sell to their families and friends. Companies that offer battery sale fundraisers include Medic Batteries + (www.medicbatteries.com/fundraising), Battery Specialists (abatterystore.com), and Interstate Batteries (http://about.interstatebatteries.com/fundraising).

265. HAT SALES

Hat sales are a great fundraiser for groups whose members and supporters wear hats, such as sporting teams. Unit prices of individual hats are low and retail sale prices are high. As a result, this provides a large margin of fundraising profit. One company to consider is Arakawa Custom Hats (www.customcapcompany.com), which boasts a unit cap price of $3.29 each. If organizations sell the hats to supporters for $25, then the unit profit is $21.71 per hat or an 86% profit margin. If you are interested in knit caps, consider fundraising with Fish Knits (fishknits.com/index_files/page9.htm). They provide hats to participating causes at about 50% of the retail cost. The great thing about hat sales is that they can be successfully sold via many mediums, including web stores, tabling events, third party retailers, road side stands, and door-to-door.

266. Flip-Flop Fundraiser

Flip-flops are inexpensive to make and to resell. Organizations can either partner with a flip-flop fundraising program or simply purchase them through a manufacturer. I recommend getting quotes from both before selecting the ideal path for an organization. Some flip-flop fundraising programs include Fan Flips (www.fanflips.com), Custom Logo Flip Flops (www.customlogoflipflops.com/ fundraiser_flipflops.html), and Bagus Custom Sandals (www.bagus custom.com). Manufacturers include ToeGuz (www.toegoz.com), 4Imprint (www.4imprint.com), and Logo Flip Flops to Go (www.logoflipflopstogo.com). Neet Feet offers both a fundraising program and standard custom flip flop orders (www.neetfeet.com).

Flip flops are a superb fundraiser for water based groups, like swim teams and polar bear clubs. Flip flops make a great donation incentive or thank you gift because of their inexpensive unit price. Consider selling them at beach side stands, at high schools and colleges, or other places flip flops are popular.

267. Slippers

A unique and rare fundraiser is the slipper sales fundraiser. This is great for around the winter holidays when families buy new pajamas and lots of gifts. One major slipper company offers a fundraising program, Happy Feet (www.buyhappyfeet.com/Fundraising-Affiliates). Most of their slippers cost between $20 and $25. They do not require any upfront deposit of funds to participate. More information is available on their website.

268. Nonprofit's Performance CD

Bands, vocalists, and other audio performers can sell their own musical performances to make a profit and promote the group. Inexpensive recording equipment can be purchased or borrowed. Organizations can burn and sell their own CDs complete with cover art or, if they do not have staff support, they can save time by using a commercial CD producer such as Superdups (superdups.com). Unit prices are low and the profit margin is high. Consider selling CDs at tables or concessions at events and performances. Ask local retailers to carry the CD as a way to support the organization. Have members buy copies as gifts and sell copies to family and friends to support the group.

269. NONPROFIT'S PERFORMANCE MP3

Selling digital media can be faster and easier. Use services like iTunes (itunes.com), Boost (boostindependentmusic.com), and Garage Band (garageband.com) to sell the nonprofit's audio performances online. Profits margins vary, and are typically about 40%. There is no individual unit cost associated with the purchase of the product, so organizations can price the digital media at a discount over the physical CDs. The organization shares its music and message with consumers around the world. The downside is that if the purchaser is not buying the music through the organization's own web store, then the group will not get the opportunity to further engage consumers by enlisting them as volunteers, soliciting additional donations, or inviting them to future events.

270. MUSIC CDS AND MP3S

The sale of recorded music is not limited to organizations that produce it themselves. Several companies provide fundraising opportunities through the sale of other artists' music. Kid Music offers personalized music and songs for children via their fundraising program (www.kidmusic.com/cgi-bin/category/fundraising). Profits vary. The advantage of Kid Music is it allows for physical CD and online sales through an organization-specific website. Charity CDs offers the organization a CD with a 20 artist compilation for $4.98 and the suggested retail price of $15 (www.charitycds.com). This represents a $10.02 profit per CD sold or a 66% profit margin. An additional plus of this program is that it provides promotional materials and information in numerous languages.

271. RELIGIOUS CD OR MP3 FUNDRAISER

For churches or youth groups, the sale of religious audio entertainment can provide a topical and successful fundraising event. Peaceful Moments Fundraising offers spiritual music via CD with a 50% profit margin to the cause (apeacefulmoment.com). Music varies from hymnals to lullabies. The Rosary on CD offers a recording of the rosary to be sold in bulk to groups and then resold by them at a profit (rosaryoncd.com). A similar program, Bibles on DVD, offers an online affiliate program where website referrals build income for other organizations (http://www.biblesondvd.com/affiliateInfo.asp).

272. SPECIAL EVENT DVD

Special event DVDs are a fantastic fundraiser for organizations like student groups. A videographer records an event and then uses editing software to produce a special event DVD. Cover art is added. Mark ups are huge on this type of fundraiser and sales are numerous, too. An example would be a student government association who hires the sole videographer for the prom and then uses that film to make a special event DVD. The DVD is then purchased by students, parents, and educators. There are numerous local videographers in most areas, so get at least five quotes before selecting a partner. Organizations may be able to find companies that will donate their services to the school and cover the expenses in order to plug their business to the community.

273. BOOK

For organizations with a very specific mission, selling or reselling a book on their topic of interest is an easy fundraiser. The organization simply buys the book at wholesale from the publisher, then makes it available via their web store and at events. An example of this is professional associations who sell authors' books on specific professional skills and certification training. Search online for books that seem to serve the organization's population. Then have multiple stakeholders, including directors and board members, review and approve the book before discussing selling it with the publisher. The publisher can guide the organization on the correct price point for the book. Profits margins are typically 50%.

274. BOOK SALE OR BOOK FAIR

A book sale is a short term book store operation. It typically lasts from 2 to 7 days. It is possible to coordinate a book sale through publishers like Usborne Canada (www.usborne.ca) or through specific book sale fundraising companies, such as Operation Bookworm (www.operationbookworm.com/pta.htm). Whichever corporate partner the organization chooses, remember to consider shipping on unsold books and any upfront costs as part of the expense of the program. Some organizations further supplement their sales by selling school supplies and book covers. Book covers can be homemade or purchased through fundraising programs like Book Ease (www.book-ease.com/fundraisers.html).

275. USED BOOK SALE

A used book sale is a great way for many different types of organizations to raise funds. First, the organization collects books. Then it operates a special sale, often over a weekend, but it could reasonably last up to a week. There are no fundraising costs because the books are donated and volunteers organize and operate the event. The event should be held at the organization's facilities or in other free space. Profits are lower than with new books sales or book fairs because the public is willing to pay significantly less for a used book than for a new one. A great time to hold a book sale of any kind is in the late spring, as avid readers begin to collect books for their summer reading list.

276. BOOKSTORE

Some organizations, such as universities, colleges, and religious groups, find that operating their own independent bookstore provides them with the opportunity to educate the public and increase revenue. Universities typically sell textbooks, books by faculty, and bestsellers. Religious groups tend to carry a wide range of books that reflect their particular religious leaning. When deciding if an organization should open a bookstore, compare the projected net store income to the income from leasing the space to a commercial bookstore or other company.

277. PASTA

Dry pasta is a popular grocery store purchase. As a result, it is perceived to be a practical thing to buy to support a nonprofit organization. Instead of purchasing bulk whole sale pasta and reselling it, consider partnering with a fundraising program like Fun Pasta Fundraising (www.funpastafundraising.com). Fun Pasta Fundraising offers silly pasta shapes that are great for gifting and a 40% to 50% profit margin for nonprofit organizations.

Some particularly lucky organizations may have volunteer chefs available to them who can make pasta for the purpose of reselling. This can increase the profit margin but adds significantly to the work and time commitment.

In addition to the traditional methods, another way to sell pasta is for organizations to have it for sale at spaghetti dinners or other special events. Selling it in and outside of grocery stores can also be very effective. It is faster than door-to-door sales and typically more successful.

278. SERVICE TRIP

Service trips take individual volunteers and have them travel to a place in need to do volunteer work. They raise funds to cover the cost of their travel and to supplement the organization's expenses. One of the most well-known service trip coordinators is Habitat for Humanity International's Global Village Program (www.habitat.org/gv/default.aspx). Each trip has a cost that varies from $1000 to $2500 and does not include airfare. Participants are encouraged to raise the funds, or they can simply donate the cost of the trip. The advantage of having participants fundraise is that they spread issue and organization awareness and further spur stewardship in their community.

Organizing a service trip program is not easy. However, if an organization already travels to developing counties to do service work, the prospect having more volunteers help and more funds may be worth the increased liability insurance and administrative time. Small organizations can realistically organize these trips. An example would be Asha Trust which plans frequent service trips to help elementary schools and provide support to the poor in Sri Lanka (www.ashatrust.co.uk). For smaller organizations, the income they receive from the trips pales in comparison to the value provided by creating strong bonds with volunteers. These relationships are maintained and long term support and volunteer relationships sustain the group into the future.

279. EDUCATIONAL TOURS

Educational tours are trips to often exotic places where participants learn about culture, conservation, and a cause. Participants pay for the privilege and the organization is supported. An illustration of an organization that has successfully provided these types of trips for years would be the New Community Project (newcommunityproject.org/learningtours.shtml). Despite having a small staff size, the New Community Project is able to consistently offer learning tours to places like the Amazon, Burma, Sudan, and Arctic Village, Alaska. These trips cost less to participate in than service trips and serve a slightly different purpose: to further cross-cultural appreciation and instill a sense of global responsibility and solidarity in participants. By working with local partners, organizations can plan educational tours to help boost fundraising income and to identify and foster relationships with future volunteers and donors.

280. PHOTO ALBUMS

Professionally-bound photo albums are a fantastic fundraiser for organizations that take service or educational trips. They can be filled with staff and volunteer pictures of their travels. Make sure that volunteers sign a release form for the use of their pictures. Albums will be purchased by organization supporters, travelers, volunteers, family and friends of volunteers, individuals from the regions depicted in the photos, and individuals who appreciate art. They can be sold via volunteer fundraisers, staff, the organization's web store, bookstores, and other retailers. The profit is considerable as long as the organization is able to sell its entire inventory.

281. Framed Photography

Taking a truly breathtaking and meaningful photo, enlarging it, and framing it is a fantastic fundraiser for organizations that do international work. Photography can be sold through interior designers, commercial decorators, galleries, the cause's web store, volunteer fundraisers, and the organization's staff. The cost of frames varies wildly, so look for companies or professionals who are willing to do high quality framing for the organization for free or at cost. Add plaques to the pieces that explain the photo including the location, photographer, and name of the organization. This will add value and serve as a plug for the organization and its international work. Consider selling low cost prints at a smaller size, such as 8'10", via the web store. Only print them after the order has been placed.

282. Commercial Trip Referrals

Some for-profit commercial companies provide organizations with a referral fee for consumers who buy tickets via a third party referral service. Fundraising Safari provides organizations who sell trips with $500 per participant (fundraisingsafari.8m.com). Cruise lines give group discounts to charities. This means that the money that individuals would save buy buying as a group goes to the organization to plan the trip. Information about this program is available online (www.benefitcruise.com). The individual margins on these types of fundraisers are very low. It is generally not worth and administrators time to dedicate to this type of fundraiser unless a large group of organization supporters chooses to participate.

283. Charity Vacations

Charity vacations are when an organization plans a vacation, charges for participation, and then manages the activities on the vacation. This works great if the organization has professional staff that can handle the administration and planning involved. Great groups for this type of fundraiser include outdoors associations, couples clubs, alumni, religious or family groups. These events build comradery among members and serve to build stronger ties with the organizing cause. Many universities and fraternal organizations coordinate annual alumni travel.

If an organization does not have any staff members that are skilled in travel planning, look for volunteers in the travel industry who can help. Survey the organization's membership to see if there is interest in a trip. If there is, ask for guidance regarding ideal dates and destinations.

284. Plant Sales

Plant sales are events where donors give potted plants, including both vegetables and flowers, to the organization to sell. These goods are then sold by volunteers, and all the proceeds go to the charity. Many groups, such as Parent Teacher Organizations and neighborhood associations, can easily organize and operate a plant sale.

Operate the sale in free space with access to free water and a hose, potentially, a parking lot outside a school or other community area. Have donors bring healthy plants, ideally perennials. Organize the sale by price point. Trees and other expensive goods should be in a separate area. Clearly mark prices. Volunteers doing the selling should be easily distinguishable by wearing matching aprons and/or hats. If possible, sell gardening supplies such as equipment and seeds if they can be donated as well. The more goods the organization offers for sale, the more the organization can make.

285. Candles

Candles are a popular gift, and as a result, generally an easy sale for a nonprofit organization. Organizations can make their own candles, purchase candles from a wholesaler, or work with a commercial fundraising program. Consider the financial and time commitment of each before choosing a path. Instructions on making candles are readily available online. Contact candle wholesalers to get a bulk purchase price.

There are many for-profit companies that offer candle sale fundraisers. Here are some companies and the profit margins they report on their websites:

- T-Bar Candle Company, 45% to 50% profit margin (www.tbarcandlecompany.com)

- The First Lady Boutique Candle Creations, 40% profit margin (www.thefirstladyboutique.com/FUNDRAISING.html)

- Honey Hand Crafts, 35% profit margin (www.honeyhivehandcrafts.com/fundraiser.html)

- Yellow Rose Gifts, Company, 40% profit margin (www.yellowrosegiftsco.com/Fundraising.html)

- Candle Cottage, 50% profit margin (www.americanheritagesoy.com/Fundraisers.html)

- Four Seasons Scents, 50% profit margin (www.fourseasonsscents.com/Fundraising.html)

- Moss Creek Candle Company, 40% to 50% profit margin (http://mosscreekcandlecompany.com/fundraisers.aspx)

- Minnesota Soy Candle Company, 50% profit margin (www.minnesotasoycandlecompany.com/Fundraiser.html)

Products and details vary, so visit the websites for more information. Additional companies are also available online. To remain cost effective, this fundraiser should utilize volunteers for the purpose of selling goods.

286. CAMP FOR KIDS

Many organizations and companies operate camps for children in order to provide a unique summer experience. Planning a camp is like launching a new business line. Research, projects, and planning in advance are essential to success. Save money and time by thinking ahead. What strategic benefits can the camp offer children that they do not already get? Will a child's attendance at the camp be reasonably priced and scheduled for area families? What realistic costs are associated with seasonal staff and facility use?

The income that an organization receives from operating camps comes from the fees parents pay to send their children there. Typically, price cuts are made for multiple children of the same family attending. Some camps already provide returning child discounts, referral discounts, and early commitment discounts. Research competitors' pricing models to determine typical rates for your market.

The biggest challenge will be securing lodging for the children while they are at the camp. Look into spaces available for rent or purchase. Commercial realtors might be able to assist with this very specific search. In many cases, liability insurance can be cost prohibitive, so speak to an insurer before opening up shop.

287. DAY CAMP FOR KIDS

A large part of the camp experience for children is the activities offered to them. Games, team building experiences, skits, crafts, and sports are often all a part of the camp experience. Day camps offer all of those things without the overnight or long distance commitment.

Many youth organizations put on day camps over the summer, winter, and other holiday breaks from school. They provide a safe place for children to learn and grow while their parents are at work. The camps are a great source of income to the organization and provide seasonal work for university students.

Day camps charge less then overnight camps but they also save a lot of money. Children bring their own sack lunches to camp. Some camps provide an afternoon snack such as juice and crackers. When pricing the day camp tuition, consider the organization's administrative, staffing, and materials costs. If the charity does not have the space for the camp, it might be able to use local schools or religious organizations' space. Any rental fees should be calculated into the cost of the program.

Some day camps offer different end times each day to meet families' needs. For example a half day, 3:30 pm, and 5:30 pm end times might all be offered. The longer the child's day the more their parents would pay in camp costs.

Camp uniforms do not have to be a large expense for the student. They can simply be a pair of blue or khaki pants and a white polo shirt. The parents can purchase these items from any retailer they choose. The uniform positively effects students' behavior and makes it easier to identify children who might be wandering away from the group.

288. Lock-In

Lock-ins are fundraising events where participants get locked into a building and stay overnight. They leave the next day. These are common fundraisers among religious organizations, but they can also be successful with really organized parent groups and libraries. Each participant in the lock-in provides a donation for the night. The donation covers their dinner, entertainment, and breakfast the next morning. The children are supervised by parent volunteers.

Organizers should plan activities in advance and be as organized as possible. The food served is often pizza for dinner and cereal for breakfast. Entertainment includes games, crafts, indoor sports, and movies appropriate for all ages. Games and movies may be free if borrowed from a local library or school. If space is owned by the organization or donated, the event can be a very large fundraiser. Organizations may want to do a series of lock-ins for different ages and genders to make it easier for volunteers and staff members to manage.

289. Wilderness Camping

Conservation and park groups may use wilderness camping as a way to raise funds. Campers pay a fee to camp and have access to the grounds. Firewood and other supplies may be sold at the office to further supplement the fundraising income. Much like a hotel, there is a check-out time by which a camper needs to leave, or be charged for an additional day. Some campgrounds include showers, restroom facilities, and electrical hook-ups. Others market themselves as true camping experiences and do not offer any accommodations. Campground licenses or permits may be required.

List the campground on online travel and leisure websites. Many allow for free directory listings. Give information to outdoors organizations and ask them to help spread the word. Offer off-season discounts through a printable online flier and send it to outdoor shops and recreation retailers. Partner with other area attractions to display each other's brochures to guests.

290. HIKING TOURS

Hiking tours are a great way to raise money while providing exercise and entertainment. Organizations like conservation groups can lead tours through parks on topics from seasonal vegetation to edible plants. Organizations charge per participant and have the tours led by volunteers, the use of whom supplements income without a per-unit cost. Off-season discounts will keep participants hiking all year long.

Many groups can benefit from the educational opportunity that a hiking tour provides. Promote the tours to clubs and businesses related to the outdoors. Also, contact area schools and children's clubs and suggest the tours as a possible field trip. Families can be invited to participate in tours as a way to have a fun and inexpensive day out. The more groups that know about the tours, the more likely they are to bring in significant income.

291. COFFEE AND TEA SALES

Two of the most consumed goods on the planet are coffee and tea. As a result, they can comprise an easy-to-sell fundraiser. If an organization chooses to partner with a fundraising company, there are numerous options. School Spirit Coffee (www.schoolspiritcoffee.com), David James Gourmet Coffee (www.davidjamescoffee.com) and Rock Solid Coffee Company (www.rocksolidcoffee.com/raise_funds.html) are examples of these. Alternatively, an organization may choose to partner with a coffee wholesaler that has a fundraising program as part of its market presence. Some of these companies include Olympic Crest Coffee Roasters (www.olycrest.com/ fundraisers.html) and Baxter Tea Company (www.baxtertea.com/mm5/merchant.mvc?Screen=FUND).

For larger communities that have local roasters, consider reaching out to them to request they provide their coffee or tea at wholesale prices for resale through the fundraiser. The organization may save on shipping and be able to increase sales by using a well-known local brand.

Coffee and tea can easily be sold through many fundraising channels. These include tabling, door-to-door sales, booths, a web store, roadside stands and retailers. The more legitimate the avenue of sales, the more likely a consumer is to make the purchase. As a result, it is helpful if volunteers wear organization t-shirts while making the sales.

292. Cosmetics

Cosmetic sales are a challenging way to raise money. It is time intensive to make the sale and many consumers do not make impulse purchases of makeup. However, if an organization has access to women above the age of 25 then it is possible for a cosmetic fundraiser to produce income. Some consumers find the use of cosmetics to be offensive or oppressive to women, so before choosing a cosmetic sale fundraiser, determine if the idea of cosmetics is in tandem with the mission and culture of the organization. Some makeup lines that offer sales based fundraising programs include Choice Aularale (www.choice-aularale.com), The Bath Divas (www.thebathdivas.com/category_s/55.htm), Lip Teezers (www.lipteezers.com/page 04.html), and Wake UP in Make Up (www.wakeupnmakeup.com/fundraising.html).

293. Homemade Soap

Homemade soap is a thoughtful and luxurious gift. Organizations can either hold a crafting event where individuals pay to make homemade soaps they take home, or they can have volunteers make soaps to sell on the organization's behalf. Homemade soaps can be sold at a premium for a significant fundraising profit to the organization. Soap sculptures and other specialty soap goods can be made from the same materials and can take a premium price. Bubble baths and liquid soap can be put into decorative bottles and sold as a holiday gift. Inexpensive and beautiful bottles can be donated or purchased from thrift stores. There are numerous websites where instructions and ingredients for soap making can be found. I recommend sampling a recipe before procuring the ingredients in bulk and setting a manufacturing date. Print special tags that can be attached with ribbon to let purchasers know that their purchase is supporting the organization's mission.

294. COMMERCIAL SOAP

If an organization does not have the administrative time to organize the manufacture of homemade soap by volunteers, a reasonable alternative is fundraising with commercial soap. Lady Bug Blessings (www.ladybugblessings.com/Fundraisers%20.htm) and Herbaria (www.herbariasoap.com/fundraising.html) offer 50% profit margins to causes participating in their fundraising programs. Luna Bug offers a 40% to 60% profit margin depending on the product and volume ordered (www.lunabugsoap.com). Some companies offer specialty products based on the cause for which they are fundraising; the Oregon Soap Shoppe, for example, offers smell and color variations depending on the charity (handcraftedcountrysoaps.com).

295. MONTHLY BUYING CLUB

A monthly buying club is a unique fundraiser. Causes such as specific industry associations sell a (insert item here) of the month club membership. Then, their members fulfill orders each month. Supporters get to receive goods each month, manufacturers get orders, and the organization raises funds. An example would be a garlic farmers association providing consumers with a different type of garlic each month. Another example would be a crafters club sending out craft materials and instructions to club members each month. Whatever the trade association, there is a buying club right for it.

    Organizing a monthly buying club requires the talents of an organized nonprofit professional. First, the association manager must decide what product should be sold. Then, she or he must set the price point appropriate to cover manufacturer expenses. Next, the fulfillment of unique product orders must be opened up to the membership for bids. Once each month has a goods manufacturer, sales can begin.

Sales of club memberships can happen throughout the year, but they are much more likely before the winter holidays. Enlist the help of members and manufacturers in promoting the program. As the club increases buyers, the manufacturers build income. A separate monthly buying club website is useful. It will increase the purchases of memberships in the monthly buying club and may be helpful in creating consistent online orders and a serious internet presence.

296. Retreat

A retreat is a gathering of organization members or supporters. It can be a day- or weekend-long event. Each attendee pays to attend and the money they provide is fundraising income to the organization. Food and meeting space can be donated. Marketing expenses can be covered through foundation underwriting or corporate sponsorship. Retreats can be held each year. Keep the content interesting, informative, and engaging, and retreat spaces will be sold. I have been able to organize retreats where attendance was free, but attendees committed to raising $1,000 in funds in the coming year. This made the $80 that was spent on the retreat well worth it. The key is finding the right attendees.

297. Homemade Teddy Bears

Teddy bears can be made by skilled sewers with a simple pattern, fabric, stuffing, and two buttons. Patterns are inexpensive and can be copied onto paper grocery bags for reuse. Organizations that have access to large groups of sewing members can make teddy bears and sell them.

Market prices of teddy bears range depending on their size and manufacturer. For lovely handmade bears sold for charity, a higher rate can be charged. Adding a Teddy Bear Birth Certificate and ribbon increases their resale value.

Teddy bears can be sold through many channels. Contact all local retailers about selling the teddy bears in their shops. Sell them via the organization's web store, events, and tabling events. If the organization is left with additional teddy bears after those efforts, then expand to door-to-door and booth sales.

298. COMMERCIALLY-PRODUCED TEDDY BEARS

Commercially-produced teddy bears are a suitable substitute for organizations without access to volunteers to do their sewing for them. Wholesale teddy bear manufacturers include Plush in a Rush (www.plushinarush.com), Ms Teddy Bear (msteddybear.us), First and Main (www.firstandmain.com), and Jo Jo (www.jojollc.com).

In additional to local manufacturers and wholesalers, there are many for-profit fundraising teddy bear programs. Some companies include BEARegards (www.bearegards.com/pages.asp?pid= fundraiser), My Signature Bear (www.mysignaturebear.com/Fund_ raising.html), and BDay Bears (www.bdaybears.com/charity-bears.html). Margins vary, with Holy Bears on the high end at 50% profit (http://www.holybears.com/main.htm).

299. RECYCLE SCRAP METAL

Recycling scrap metal can forward an environmental organization's purpose, as well as bring in money. Many communities have scrap metal recycling centers where the company managing the facility will pay based on the quality and weight of the good. In addition, there are online resources which can provide information about scrap metal rates and recycling locations. These include Recycle In Me (www.recycleinme.com), National Recycling Inc (www.national recyclinginc.com), SA Recycling (www.sarecycling.com), and the Institute of Scrap Recycling Industries (www.isri.org).

300. TEMPORARY TOY STORE

A temporary toy store is a fundraiser where the organizing charity arranges a toy store, typically for 2 to 7 days, whose proceeds benefit the cause. Look for a free space for the store. Sometimes schools or libraries will have rooms that can be donated. Volunteers should operate the stores as retail associates. They should wear matching clothes and nametags to make them easily identifiable by customers. A business license may be required.

There are many inventory options for temporary toy stores. Temporary toy stores can be filled with new or used donated toys. They can also be filled with goods provided via wholesalers, manufacturers, or other toy stores. Another option is to use for-profit fundraising toy programs such as Calplush (www.calplush.com) and Smart Smart Toys (www.smartstarttoys.com).

Book twice as many volunteers as the store needs to run. This will prevent being short-staffed. Use the charity's credit card machine to process credit card purchase. Price tags can be inexpensively added simply by writing with sharpie on masking tape or professional looking tags can be printed that include the organization's logo and read, "This toy benefits (insert cause here)." I recommend posting multiple signs that inform customers that there are absolutely no returns or personal checks accepted due to the temporary nature of the store. Consider operating the temporary toy store right before the kick-off of the winter holiday shopping season. This fundraiser is particularly appropriate for causes focused on minors, such as a children's hospital.

301. SAUCES

Sauces aren't just a family tradition. They are also a fundraiser! They can be sold via tabling events, grocery stores, realtors, cook-offs or other special events, and web stores. If the organization has access to a free commercial kitchen, it may be able to make its own sauces for a reasonable price. An alternative is to ask supporters to make sauces. However, because all-natural sauces are not shelf stable, homemade sauces that are continuously refrigerated can cause food poisoning. Organizations can purchase sauces from wholesalers and sell at retail prices for a profit. This is a particularly attractive strategy if there is a local brand of sauces.

If none of these product procurement plans work well for the organization, then consider a for-profit sauce fundraising program. Here are several along with their advertised profit margins:

- A Little Dip Will Do Ya!, 40% to 50% Profit Margins (dipfundraiser.com)

- The Crimson Lion, 50% Profit Margins (www.thecrimsonlion.com/wholesale_fundraisingsauces.html)

- Galena Dips, 50% to 100% Profit Margins (galenadips.com/fundraising.html)

- The Glen Farms Grape Vine, Margins not reported (www.glenfarmsgourmet.com/Fundraising.htm)

- Bill's Black Label Barbeque Sauce, Profit Margin Varies (www.billsblacklabel.com/BBQSauce_Fundraising.html)

- Sugar n' Spice, Margins not reported (sugarnspiceinc.com/fundraising_step_by_step.html)

- Scoville Hot Sauce, Margins not reported (www.hotsauceprivatelabel.com)

- Columbus Fundraising, 50% Profit Margin (www.columbusfundraising.com/salsaandbbqsaucefundraiser.htm)

Products, customer support, and shipping costs vary, so review individual websites before selecting a commercial partner.

302. YARD DECORATIONS

Renting yard decorations is a fun activity that can build awareness of an organization and provide income. If an organization promotes art, especially youth artists, then this might be the ideal fundraising activity. Generally yard decorations take the form of painted plywood cut outs. They are placed in a person's yard to celebrate their accomplishments or celebrations. Birthdays, birth announcements, weddings, graduations, and awards are all popular reasons for people to display yard decorations.

The cutouts should be made by a professional wood craftsperson or carpenter. However, the painting can be done by volunteers and organization members. Individuals pay for the decorations to be put in their own or a friend's yards for a week at a time. Volunteers place them and then remove them and return them to storage.

If an organization is not able to make high-quality yard decorations, it may be able to get them donated by area businesses. Be creative as to what can decorate the yard. A flock of pink flamingos are a popular decoration. Flamingo Fundraising offers these as a fundraising program (www.flamingofundraising.com). Organizations can also purchase or have donated party or holiday decorations and reuse those.

Once the program and materials have been chosen, use word of mouth to push sales. Make a program sign that advertises the fundraiser. Then, put it in various members' yards along with decorations throughout the course of several weeks until customers come forward. This will quickly let the area community known about the program without the expense of purchasing advertising space. Make sure there is plenty of information about the program and decoration options on the organization's website.

303. Basketball Tournaments

Basketball tournaments are good fundraisers for sports organizations, schools, and youth centers. Give the tournament an exciting name. Two-on-Two or Three-on-Three tournaments are easy to recruit teams for. Plan the tournament a year in advance. This will allow plenty of time for recruitment of players and volunteers. If all of the individuals who serve at the event are volunteers, then the overhead costs can stay low. Teams pay to play, and spectators pay a small fee for seats and concessions.

The organization should use its facilities or park basketball courts for the tournament. Recruit volunteer referees. Trophies and prizes are given to the top teams in each category of play. Categories can include women 18 and under, men 18 and under, co-ed 18 to 60, co-ed 61 and over. Costs are at a minimum for this fundraiser, so income can be maximized. Holding this event each year will help increase awareness and participation in it.

Send out press releases about the game schedule and the winners in each bracket. Try to secure local media coverage of the winning game. Keep track of rankings from year to year. Make them available on the organization's website to promote competition. Also use them to better match up players the following year.

304. POPCORN

Popcorn and decorative tins are popular gifts, especially among colleagues. Popcorn can be sold by many organizations, but volunteer fundraisers should be utilized to keep the fundraiser costs low. Popcorn can easily be sold as a door-to-door fundraiser, via tabling, and as an in-store sale. There are numerous companies that offer popcorn fundraising programs. Some of these include Snappy Popcorn (www.snappypopcorn.com/ProductCart/pc/fundraising.asp), Rural Route 1 Popcorn (www.ruralroute1.com/fundraising.asp), Col. Pop's Popcorn (www.colpops.com/fundraisers.php), Krazy for Korn (www.krazy4korn.ca/Getting%20Started.htm), Popcorn Palace (popcornpalace.com/Home/Fundraising), and Catoctin Popcorn (catoctinpopcorn.com/Fundraising_information.aspx).

In addition to selling tins of popcorn, a fantastic way to build quick cash is to have a party supply company donate the use of a popcorn stand machine. Then, the organization can secure corn, oil, and bags and sell it in front of a school, store, or sporting event. Fresh popped popcorn's tempting buttery smell sells itself. Volunteers can sell small bags of popcorn for $2 each and cans of soda for $1. This can bring in fistfuls of cash with minimal organization effort.

305. DANCE

Dances can be an easy way for student organizations to raise funds. First, have parents find a donated space. This can be a gymnasium, hall, or youth center. Music can be provided by volunteers. Parents chaperone the event. Each child pays to attend and to buy refreshments. Parent volunteers assist with child pick-up. This is an easy way for student organizations to increase income while furthering their relationships with children and their parents in the community.

306. Dance Class

A series of dance classes can be a great way for cultural or social organizations to build the funds while increasing their outreach in the community. A special event dance class is a way for other organizations to raise funds, as well.

At a special event dance class, an instructor teaches a dance to all attendees. After the instructional period is complete, the floor is open to dancing and music is played. An instance of such an event I attended was a Mexican cultural appreciation organization's salsa dance class. A restaurant eager for drink sales donated their large party room. Each attendee paid $20 and a volunteer taught everyone how to dance the salsa. Then, a DJ played salsa music, and the floor was open to dancing for the rest of the night. The attendance fees went to the organization.

To increase revenue, hold the event at a place where the organization can provide concessions with the help of volunteers. For a salsa class, there are companies that provide the condiment salsa as a fundraiser, Jose Madrid Salsa (salsafundraising.com/Fundraising/Fundraising.htm). Something like that could also be sold at the event in addition to concessions.

If a series of classes are offered, think through scheduling carefully. By holding the classes on the same weekend evening each week or on Saturday afternoons or evenings, the organization can sell bulk class tuitions and offer a discount to increase income.

307. Fruit

Fruit sales are a practical way to raise funds. They work for any group with volunteers doing the fundraising. Fruit can be sold in front of religious organizations, grocery stores, and community centers, or door-to-door.

Fruit can be procured through grocery distributors, farm co-ops, and area farmer donors. In the past, I have received donations from grocery distributors, grocery stores, and big box stores. Our organization's only obligation was to pick up the donations from their location. Another way to procure fruit to sell is by working with for-profit fruit fundraising programs. These tend to follow one of two models. Either volunteer fundraisers take orders from customers and then fulfill them later via the company, or they purchase the fruit up front and then sell it. With stands, it best to have fruit individuals can take home immediately. With door-to-door sales, it is best to have orders placed in advance. Either fulfillment model can work. Companies that provide fruit fundraising campaigns include: Fruit Langdon Barber Groves (www.lbg.org/Fundraising.cfm), Mixon Fruit Farms (www.mixon.com/fundraising.asp), New York Apple Association (www.nyapplecountry.com/fundraising.htm), Fresh Fruit Fundraiser (www.800apples2.com), Sun Groves (www.sungroves.com/fundraising), and The World's Best Fruit (www.theworldsbestfruit.com).

308. SALON DAY

Salon days are days that salons provide free services, and the money that would normally be charged goes to a charity. This is a popular fundraiser for women's organizations, such as ovarian cancer support groups and foundations. I have organized salon day fundraising events before, and I have found that two things make all the difference. The first and most important thing is a large number of committed volunteers to help sell services and promote the event. Second, there needs to be a way for services to be sold in advance through certificates or online purchases to make it possible to guarantee income.

309. SPA DAY

Spa days are similar to salon day events. Instead of hair services, customers may receive a wide range of spa services including facials and manicures. The advantage of a spa day is that it can be held in many different types of locations. Furthermore, volunteers can provide many of the services offered. You can increase income at a spa day by producing the products used from scratch and by selling homemade products, such as soaps, to participants. An organization can also expand its fundraising income by selling concessions like mimosas, chocolate, pizza, and other comfort foods.

This is a great fundraiser for women's groups and clubs. The larger the organization, the more attendees, and the more items sold, the more earning potential the event has. If each member of a twenty person group has three of their friends or family members attend, then that is sixty people to purchases services. If each service nets an income of $30, then the one day event would bring in $1,800! That is a pretty remarkable income from one day of pampering.

310. DOG TAGS

Dog tags sales constitute a fundraiser whereby the product price and resale price are low. As a result, an organization will need to sell an incredibly high volume of dog tags for the fundraiser to be successful. Wholesale dog tags are inexpensively available starting at $0.46 per tag. The unit price goes up when orders are small or tags have many colors in complex patterns. Wholesalers include Wholesale Carabiners (www.wholesale-carabiners.com/custom-engraved-dog-tag.html) and logo tags (www.logotags.com). One dog tag fundraising company is JROTC Dog Tags (www.jrotcdogtags.com/fundraising.htm). While income potential for small organizations is low, dog tags can build comradery among supporters and awareness about an organization. As a result, dog tag sales have an added benefit to an organization that sales of other consumable items, such as fruit, do not have.

311. PERSONALIZED GAMES

Personalized games can provide a unique keepsake for organization supporters looking to help a cause. Many companies provide personalized games made-to-order, as well as games that individuals take home and personalize. Two companies to consider are Enginuity (www.enginuity.com) and Custom Board Games (www.custom boardgames.com).

To increase volunteers' involvement in the fundraiser, ask them to create a game. They write the rules. The game can use any materials easily obtainable by the organization, such as a standard deck of cards or dice. Then, the volunteers design box cover art. The organization packages and sells the games. This increases profit over that made from professionally customized games. It also increases the likelihood that volunteers will buy one or more games.

312. MEMORY CARD GAME

For the less ambitious game master, a game of memory can be an easy and very personalized fundraiser. Organizations with many photos can use the photos to print cards. Other groups can have members draw pictures. The cards have the organization's logo on one side and the photo or other picture on the other. There should be two copies of each image in each deck. Decks should have at least 50 cards. The more cards they have, the more expensive the game is to produce and the more challenging the memory card game will be.

To play Memory, a person shuffles the deck and deals all the cards face down. Players take turns turning over two cards at a time. If the two cards match they pick them up and play again. If they do not match, the player turns them both back over. When all the cards are picked up the player with the most sets of matching cards wins. These instructions should be printed out, along with the organization's information, for each deck sold.

Memory cards are a great fundraiser for groups that support children or who have members that are children. While the decks are more expensive to produce than buying a simple standard deck of cards, they are personalized and the profit goes to a charity. If members do the decorating of the cards, they are more likely to buy decks and help sell them to their friends. Other channels for sales are web stores and retailers.

313. CHARADES TOURNAMENT

Charades tournaments are a fun and fantastic fundraiser for religious groups, community centers, and parent associations. Any groups with adult members or families can make a charades tournament a success. In fact, many games make great tournaments. However, charades requires no equipment or permission from the copyright owner. Also, charades is a popular game, and many individuals know the basic rules.

In organizing a charades tournament, find a free space for play. This can be a member's home, the organization's office, space at a religious organization, or a community center. Then determine team size and make up. Having charades teams of two makes it easy to find teams to participate.

Set an entry fee to compete. This is the primary source of income. The entry fee should be around $10 per person or $20 for a two person team. Refreshments and souvenirs can be sold at the event for additional income. Other income-generating activities, such as fundraising sales, can be happening the same day to further increase revenue.

The three top teams should receive trophies. These can be donated or purchased through event sponsorship funds. The grand champion should get a special prize that could include a gift basket of donated goodies.

314. PILLOWCASE SALE

Pillowcases are one of the simplest sewing projects available. Organizations that are particularly likely to make a pillowcase sale a success include student groups with access to school sewing machines, such as consumer science associations, or individual crafting groups. Members can then make pillowcases to sell as fundraisers. The benefit to having the craft made by young adults is that parents, community members, and friends will be eager to buy the pillowcases to support their charitable involvement, while getting something personal from the child.

Inexpensive or donated fabric and thread are all that is needed to produce a large quantity of pillowcases. Ask fabric, craft, and interior design stores to act as event sponsors for the fundraiser through the in-kind donation of materials. If organizers are concerned about the resulting pillowcases themselves, simple patterns can be made with paper grocery bags, which will help new sewers make consistent rectangles.

315. FIFTY/FIFTY RAFFLE

A fifty/fifty raffle is a fundraiser where individuals purchase tickets. Generally, the raffle ticket price is one dollar each. Then, one number is pulled and that is the winning number. The winner gets 50% of the funds raised from the raffle. Raffles and other games of chance sometimes require gambling licenses, so check with local government to see if that is applicable.

This fundraiser is a huge seller at charity events because individuals know that by the end of the night, one of them will be a winner. Some organizations are lucky enough to pull the ticket of a generous person who immediately donates their winnings back to the organization. Another way to increase sales is by having second or third place prizes of goods that are donated to the raffle. Organizations can also offer bulk ticket buying discounts, such as having 1 for $1 or 25 for $20. This provides an incentive for buyers to stock up on chances to win.

316. MAGNET FRIDGE FRAME

Magnet fridge frames are simple fundraiser items that sell well around the holidays. Great places to sell them are at retail shops and via web stores. Magnet frames can be made by individual organizations. The steps are simple. Procure, ideally through donations, printable magnet paper. Then design and print out a picture frame. This design allows for the organization to include logos and special organization messages. The frame should have rectangles and squares in the design. These rectangles and squares are cut out to create open spaces for purchasers' photos.

If magnet frames cannot be economically produced, the organization can purchase them through a wholesaler or fundraising program. One company that provides refrigerator frames as a fundraising program is Fridge Frame (fridgeframe.com/fundraising.php).

317. FACEBOOK CAUSE BIRTHDAY GIFT

Facebook offers an application that allows members to choose a cause to be their birthday gift. Friends and families can donate to that cause as a gift to the individual to celebrate that person's birthday. Your organization reaps many benefits for participating in this application:

- Receipt of donations thanks to birthday gifts

- Added awareness of cause and organization

- Identification of supporters

- Opportunity to recruit volunteers, event attendees, and future supporters

To participate in this program, organizations should set up a cause page on Facebook. Additionally, they should ask supporters via their web page, cause page, and eNewsletter to make the cause their Facebook cause birthday gift.

318. Christmas Shop

For Christian organizations with access to free retail space, a Christmas shop can be a source of significant fundraising income. Christmas shops sell Christmas holiday related goods. These are often decorations and decorative gifts. Temporary Christmas shops tend to open right before Thanksgiving and operate through Christmas Eve. Year-round Christmas shops tend to get the most business from Thanksgiving to Christmas Eve as well. The benefits of a temporary shop are that it can be staffed with volunteers, and it can institute a no return policy.

There are many ways to procure goods to sell. Goods sold can be new or used donated items. There can also be wholesale items donated or purchased from manufacturers. Other retailers may donate after-season goods that can be stored and kept for the following year's shop. Seasonal treats, including hot cocoa and coffee can be sold in the shop, too. The more goods an organization collects, the more funds will be raised. No one likes to shop in a sparsely-stocked store.

319. CHRISTMAS ORNAMENTS

Christmas ornaments programs can be good fundraisers for Christian groups, including churches. One great keepsake for families is a custom ornament. There are several companies that offer ornament fundraising programs, including Ornaments Wullbrandt Studio (www.wullbrandtstudio.com), Custom ornaments (www.fundraising ornaments.com/charityfundraising.html), and Kastle Land USA (www.kastleland.com/fundraisers.html). Other manufacturers can make customized ornaments, including Ornaments & More (www.ornamentsandmore.com), Ornament Shop (www.ornament shop.com), Russell Rhodes (www.russellrhodes.com), Customized Memories (www.customizedmemories.com), and Zazzle (www.zaz zle.com). Investigate fundraising, whole sale, and retail buying options before choosing a fundraising partner.

Using an online form for orders can streamline the fundraising process and prevent the organization from making mistakes. Use a free survey services like surveymonkey.com to collect all the data for the customized ornaments. Set the submission deadline far enough in advance so that families can collect their ornaments before Christmas. If the fundraiser is at a church, have the ornaments available for pick up at the church to save money on shipping.

320. WREATHS & CHRISTMAS TREES

Another fundraiser that can be successful for Christian groups, including churches, is wreath and Christmas tree sales. Churches can rent out part of their parking lot to a vendor to sell the wreaths and trees or they can sell them themselves. Remember that if the organization chooses to sell the trees and wreaths themselves, they will likely need to hire seasonal staff to help manage the tree sales. This dramatically adds to the overhead expenses of the fundraiser.

In additional to local wholesalers, organizations can consider working with wreath and tree fundraising programs. There are numerous potential partners, including Spates the Florist (www.spates theflorist.com), Northwoods Evergreen & Wire Company (www.northwoodevergreen.com), Nature By Design, Inc. (www.naturebydesign.com), Evergreen Industries (www.evergreen industries.net/fundraising/default.htm), Christmas Trees World

Wide (www.christmastreesww.com/fundraiser.htm), Alpine Christmas Wreaths (www.alpinewreaths.com), Vermont Center Wreaths (www.vermontcenterwreaths.com/fundraise.php), Pine River Wreath (www.pinerivertreeandwreath.com), The Cedar Rose Garden Shop (www.cedarose.ca/fundraising_wreaths.html), DeLong Farms (delongfarms.com/fund.html), Wilson Wreath (www.wilsonwreath .com/wilsonwreaths/1566/Fundraising), and Alpine Farms (www. alpinefarms.com/fundraising.html). Some of these services will allow organizations to stock inventory without a large initial upfront cost. Others will allow you to collect orders in advance and then fulfill them.

321. MAKE AND TAKE CRAFTS

Make and take crafts are crafts where customers make items from materials provided by the organization and then take them home. This is a great fundraiser for arts organization or organizations with numerous volunteer crafters. Experiential fundraisers are a great way to have supporters create a memory and thus strengthen their bond with an organization. Few things are more personal than making something out of a lump of clay and then having it fired in a kiln. Some crafts are even more instantaneous, like making jewelry or decorating picture frames. No matter the craft, the cost of the event will be in materials. The space used should be the organization's space. Materials can be purchased from wholesalers. Have attendees RSVP in advance to avoid over-purchasing.

322. BUTTONS

Buttons are a popular fundraiser among political candidates. They are also a great way to raise money for many causes. They are especially effective for organizations that have numerous supporters interested in purchasing them, because their wholesale and resale prices are low. Organizations can purchase button makers; however, it is typically more cost and time effective to purchase buttons. Buttons also work well as a supplement to other sales efforts or in web stores.

Before choosing the content of the button, consider the culture and image of the organization. Would a humorous button be appreciated by the supporters or would a simpler logo work best? Would a powerful call to action sell well, or would a simple slogan be more effective? Consider which organizational t-shirts have sold best if guidance is needed.

Once the content and approximate size have been chosen, it is time to compare quotes. Businesses that specifically make buttons for nonprofit fundraisers include Buttons of Hope (www.buttons ofhope.com), Buttons Online (www.buttonsonline.com/ fundraising_ideas.html), and Bean Town Buttons (www.beantownbuttons .com/events_fundraising_buttons.htm). There are numerous commercial companies that also provide customized wholesale buttons. These include Everyone Loves Buttons (www.everyoneloves buttons.com/), Wacky Buttons (www.wackybuttons.com), Affordable Buttons (www.affordablebuttons.com), and Button Works (www.buttonworks.com). There is also an association of US based manufacturers called Just Buttons that provides instant online quotes (www.justbuttons.org). Remember that organizations will need to take all orders in advance when dealing with most fundraising companies and all wholesalers.

323. LAPEL PINS

Lapel pins are a great choice for organizations whose supporters frequently wear business or business-casual attire. In comparison to a button, they are a smaller, more subtle sign of support. They also cost more per unit in wholesale and resale costs, so the margins are larger. As a result, they are generally a good fundraiser for organizations able to sell them at events and through a web store. Fundraising companies that provide lapel pins include Pins and Buttons (www.lapelpinandbutton.com), Custom Pins (www.custompins .com), Lapel Pin Productions (www.lapelpinproductions.com), and US Pin (uspin.net). Wholesalers include Pin Source (www.pin source.com), Pins Patch and More (www.pinspatchesandmore.com), Wholesale Pins (www.wholesalepins.com), and Quality Lapel Pins (www.qualitylapelpins.com).

324. ORGANIZATION-PRODUCED CHILDREN'S BOOK

For many causes, a children's book can be a great way to promote the organization's mission while selling goods to its primary stakeholders. Consider content carefully. Enlist volunteers to help write and illustrate the book. Make sure the message of the book is clear and cannot be misinterpreted.

Once the words and imagery have been created, determine the page length. This will help when getting price quotes for printing and binding the book. Once final copies are put together by a printer, sell the book via volunteer fundraisers, on the web store, and at organization events. Ask volunteers who helped construct the book to attend and promote signing events. This will increase the volunteers' commitment to the project and the organization, and offer an additional opportunity for sales.

325. INSTANT PLANTS

In the spring, a great fundraiser for outdoors organizations and other adult supporters is selling instant plants. These are typically pots with soil and seeds already in them. The purchaser provides water and sunlight. Eventually, the purchaser can transplant the seedling into the ground or keep it in the pot indefinitely. Herbs are popular instant plants because they are hardy perennials that grow well across North America.

Constructing the instant plants is a little bit of work for volunteers and requires the procurement of all ingredients. If organizing volunteer fundraisers to do it themselves is too much administrative hassle or will keep volunteers from purchasing the plants, then consider partnering with a greenhouse or fundraising company. Reach out to area farmers and greenhouses to see what partnerships terms they can offer. Then compare those offers to those offered by fundraising companies such as Peach State Fundraising (www.peach statefundraising.com/UNIQUEFUNDRAISERS.html).

Completed instant plants should include a label that lets purchasers know what organization they are supporting, and provides the charity's website address. Once the goods have been assembled, sell them via events, in parking lots, in front of retailers, and at greenhouses. Not every channel is appropriate for this fundraiser.

For instance, mailing plants will be messy and costly so avoid selling via web stores.

326. FRAMED MEMBERSHIP CERTIFICATES

Framed membership certificates are a great fundraiser for professional, fraternal, and alumni organizations. The organization gets contract bids for sophisticated matting and framing of certificates. A vender is then chosen. When a certificate is awarded, the organization purchases the framing of that certificate through the vendor. The vender frames and sends the certificate to the consumer. Income from this fundraiser comes from the up sell of the final product to the consumer. Frequently, the purchaser of the framed certificate is not the individual to whom it is awarded, but rather a spouse, guardian, or mentor. As a result, the purchase should be able to be placed over the phone to the organization and via the organization's web store.

327. ONLINE BOOKSTORE

Organizations that offer certifications or accreditations can provide online test preparation resources via an online bookstore. These specialty books are rarely available through alternative means, and as a result, they provide a strong fundraising option for associations. They do not require the opportunity cost to the organization brought by a physical bookstore, and they make the goods available to members worldwide. For universities, they provide an easy way for guardians to purchase books for students who might otherwise forgo their textbook purchases. College bookstores typically offer required and suggested texts for classes, additional books by faculty, and best sellers. Online bookstores do not have the overhead costs of maintaining a large inventory, goods damaged by shoppers, and large staffs.

328. JEWELRY

Jewelry sales are an opportunity for organizations to fundraise via online orders and door-to-door advance orders. Volunteer fundraisers should be utilized for jewelry sales due to the high level of time required to secure sales. Many organizations can benefit from this fundraiser; however, it is ideal for organizations whose members and supporters are adults with disposable income. It is most effective if held before the winter holidays or for Valentine's Day.

There are several businesses that offer jewelry sales fundraisers. These include All Sport Jewelry (www.allsportjewelry.com), Glimmers (www.glimmersinc.com/c-8-fundraising.aspx), Ring U (www.ring-u.com/index.php?p=1_7_Fundraising), WOW Imports (www.wow-imports.com/personalized-jewelry-fundraiser.asp), and Rock Paper Scissors (www.rpsetc.com). Products, fees, margins, and customer support vary. Some companies provide very personalized jewelry items that are organization-specific. Others offer pieces that have general consumer appeal. Consider the modes of sales and potential customers before selecting the right fundraising partner. Wholesale companies are also plentiful. They include All Tribes (www.alltribes.com), Blanka Diamonds (www.blankadiamonds.be), Fancy Beads (www.fancybeads.com), Kingdom Wear (www.kingdomwear.com), Silver Source (www.silversource.com), and Touch of Avalon (www.touchofavalon.com).

Whenever doing nonprofit sales for pricey or customized items, remember to collect the orders and money in advance of placing the purchase order with the fundraising company or wholesaler. This will prevent organizations from losing money on goods that they cannot easily resell when the original customer does not pay for the good or is no longer interested in it. To save money on shipping and goods delivery, email and/or phone individuals who have placed orders and ask them to come to the organization's office sometime during a two-day period to collect the goods. Extend the office hours slightly on those days, and have staff members and/or volunteers check identifications and hand out goods. This will save the time and money of providing shipping or delivery. Consumers may be excited to get their goods sooner, too.

329. WALK

Fundraising walks are a massively successful way for causes with large community support to build awareness and fundraising income. There are famous and infamous walk fundraisers. They vary in length and fundraising requirements. However, there are several details in planning a walk that I have found make a significant difference regardless of the cause.

First, select a location that is easily accessible by public transportation and automobile. This will maximize attendance. If the organization is able to afford to hold the event at a destination, then that is even better. Liability insurance is a must for special events. Make sure to have a certificate of event insurance present at the walk.

Second, use fundraising software to accept registrations and donations before the walk. In my experience, a well-promoted walk can reach its fundraising goal before the walk even starts if an easy-to-use registration and fundraising website is in place. Use the email addresses that are received through the online registration to send walk information and fundraising tips out to participants. Also allow individuals to turn in donations and register at the event.

Finally, for the day of the walk, organize volunteer speakers, programming, and even music. Keep the event's activities going throughout the duration of the walk. Make sure that all programming is appropriate for the occasion. For instance, if it is a somber affair, arena music should not be played.

After the event results are in, send a thank you to participants with the results. Make sure that volunteers get a special thank you. The number of volunteers needed to run the event is typically 10% of the total attendees. If it is possible, thank volunteers and event chairpersons by name.

330. PARADE FLOAT

Parade floats can be a fantastic way to promote an organization and spur donations. Organizations that typically have floats include membership groups, political parties, and school organizations. Organizations should consider participating in any parade in their areas of operation which are free for them to participate in.

Floats are typically decorated wagons pulled by tractors or trucks. Reusable flowers can be made to cover the float from plastic trash bags and wire. Simple instructions and kits can be found online.

Volunteers do not have to be skilled carpenters to create parade floats. For instance, I once saw a nonprofit volunteer service organization participate in a parade by having members dress up in organization t-shirts and push brooms down the parade path.

331. PARADE

For the more ambitious charity, organizing an entire parade can offer an opportunity to very publicly promote the cause and raise funds. Organizations that typically organize parades include tourism boards, neighborhood associations, and minority rights groups.

Organizing a parade begins with getting permits for the event approved by the municipality. The approval may require a deposit, other fees, and/or signatures from community members. Then, find area associations and businesses willing to participate. It is common to charge a fee for participation in the parade. This fee usually varies based on the size and media coverage of the event, and whether the participating group is a for-profit or not-for-profit organization. To further encourage participation, offer awards for the best floats. To further increase attendance, make the parade an annual event and hold it on a weekend. Entrance to the parade should be free. Booths and other commercial sources of revenue can increase fundraising.

An announcer with sound equipment should be stationed near the stands. Outdoor speakers should carrier the announcer's voice to the crowd. This will allow the announcer the opportunity to introduce each party as it goes by.

The parade should be led by a Grand Marshall. The Grand Marshall should be a public figure that supports the cause and is well-known in the area. If the parade is a children's parade organized by a children's hospital, then the Grand Marshall could be a character in costume. If the parade celebrates a community's heritage, then a well-loved member of that community should serve as the Marshall.

332. SOUVENIR BALL

Organizations that support sports teams, such as Parent Teacher Associations or Booster Clubs, might find that souvenir ball sales produce consistent income from parents of participants. Souvenir balls are sports memorabilia that are personalized for the team. An example of this would be a volleyball in the colors of the team with a group photo of the team on it. Souvenir balls typically offer margins of 50%. In primary and high schools, balls should be paid for in advance of the order being placed. For colleges or universities, the balls should be ordered and sold at sporting events and via the organization's web store.

Companies that manufacture souvenir balls include Photo Ball (www.photoball.com), Soccor Promotion (www.soccer-promotion.com), Vieoco Balloons (www.viecoballoons.com/mini sport.htm), and Best Coach Gifts (www.bestcoachgifts.com). Prices vary. Some balls come with trophy-like holders that are ideal for displaying the ball. Player gift packages can also be put together for parents to purchase that include personalized sports bags.

333. PERSONALIZED PUZZLE

For organizations with a large number of members, a fundraiser aimed at members and their loved ones could be selling personalized puzzles with the group's photo on them. For organizations who operate in exotic places, puzzles with photos of their tours and travels might sell well among supporters.

One company that I have used extensively for photo puzzle gifts is Portrait Puzzles (www.portraitpuzzles.com). They provide a box with the photo on the top for free and a variety of size and price options. There are numerous other photo puzzle providers who make smaller souvenir puzzles which are less for true puzzling and more for gift giving. No matter the partner chosen, ask for a nonprofit and bulk buying discount. Do not forget to show proof of 501C3 status to have sales tax waived.

Whichever vendor is chosen, be selective with the photo. Remember that the picture will likely be blown up many times, and so be conscious of the photo's resolution. Also remember that the more objectively eye-catching and beautiful the picture, the more likely the puzzle is to sell. For example, animal shelters may choose to put an adorable photo of a kitchen and puppy sleeping beside each other on their puzzle. A conservation organization may choose to use a particularly stirring photo of the Amazon or Arctic tundra. Organizations may choose to produce more than one puzzle at a time.

Sales of puzzles can be done via many different channels. Obviously, they can be sold at the organization's office and via its web store. Additionally, they should be available for sale at organization events, through tabling activities, and at retailers. If boxes are still left over after the campaign ends, ask supporters to sell them door-to-door or at roadside stands.

Make sure every box clearly states that the purchase of the puzzle benefits the cause. Include information about the cause and how to make charitable donations directly to the organization. Organizations should put information about the photo itself in the box as well.

334. Cross-country Walk

In recent years, several causes have reached a national audience with their messages by having cross-country walks. These are walks where one person or a few supporters walks from one side of the country to another. Cross-county walk campaigns have focused on issues including children aging out of foster care, diabetes and obesity, and issues of taxation.

Many organizations' typical officers and directors coverage does not cover activities and events outside of the facility or state. Special liability insurance coverage is essential for a cross-country walk. Cross-county walks can be physically dangerous, especially if the walk participants move through areas not typically appropriate for walking or camping out.

The key to a successful cross-county walk is event promotion. Walkers should have continuous access to social media. Additionally, volunteers throughout the country should help to organize local press and repost the walkers' progress. The more volunteers engaged with online and local media, the more coverage the walk will get and the more attention and donations the cause will receive.

335. Religious Goods Sale

For religious organizations, selling goods themed to their celebrations and traditions is a unique way to raise funds while promoting their spiritual community. Many religious groups have members who are crafts people: these individuals can make goods to sell. Members may also have things they are willing to donate that they do not need and may have never used.

Goods can be sold at the religious center and via the organization's web store. The larger the community, the more donors will come forward, and the more consumers will be available to shop at the sale. The more goods available to sell to attendees, the higher the fundraising income will be.

If an organization is not able to get enough goods donated for the sale, it can partner with wholesalers or fundraising programs. Some of these include Rebel (jesusisarebel.com/home.html), Happy Mail (www.happymailinc.com/fundraising.asp), In Your Faith (www.inyourfaith.net/groupfundraising.html), and Holy Land Mall (www.holylandmall.net). Many of these vendors require an organization to purchase the goods before shipments are made. As a result, organizations can either have orders placed in advance or keep store items that do not sell and attempt to sell them the following year.

336. GIVING TREE

A giving tree fundraiser is a philanthropic campaign where a large tree is placed in a frequently viewed area. It includes a trunk and branches coming up from the ground. Supporters donate and get their name on leaves that are placed on the tree. Campaigns frequently have messages like "Show your roots" or "Help Us Grow."

A set amount is required as a minimum donation to get a leaf placed on the tree. When determining what the set minimum donation should be, think about the following things:

• The cost per leaf for the campaign including the cost for the engraved leaf

• The total fundraising goal of the campaign

• How much each member would need to give to reach that goal if 25% of members or supporters participated in the campaign

• What a realistic and attainable donation goal is to maximize participation

Once the minimum donation for the leaf is set, begin to promote the fundraiser via word of mouth, a plaque by the tree, special announcements, the newsletter and/or e-newsletter, the website, and press releases. Public knowledge of the giving tree and repeated reminders about it are essential to maximizing its success.

337. Yard Work

Yard work is a tiresome task. For organizations with members who live in areas where green spaces are common, a yard work fundraiser is a great way to spread the word and raise funds. This is especially effective for organizations like sports team and school clubs. Children should be supervised and assisted by guardians.

Members take informational fliers door-to-door and offer to do yard work, such as raking leaves, in exchange for a minimum donation to the organization. The donor can make out the check directly to the organization. The amount of the minimum donation depends on the amount of time the work will take to do. Tips go directly to the organization, too.

Volunteers should bring their own rakes and other supplies with them. This fundraiser is great because the only costs are the fliers. To increase the amount of funds raised, ask each participant to set a specific and realistic fundraising goal for themselves. This goal will be for the purpose of motivation only.

338. Plow for a Purpose

For organizations whose volunteers have access to snow plows, a quick way to raise a lot of funds is to offer a plow for a purpose program. Individuals get their driveways plowed and then donate the cost of the plowing to the specific cause for which the volunteer is raising funds. A great way to promote this fundraiser is to post signs by major roadways and intersections. Expenses are covered by volunteers, so organizations stand to make significant funds.

339. GO-CART RACE

Go-cart races are fun ways for organizations to raise funds. Individuals pay to compete and race. The winners receive trophies. This fundraiser works best when organizations have a large network of supporters ages 18-55. A key to making this fundraiser cost effective is to get a go-cart racing facility to donate the use of their carts and facility for the races. Have each racer sign a waiver of liability and get additional liability insurance for the event.

340. COOKIE EXCHANGE

A cookie exchange is a fundraiser where each attendee brings a dozen homemade cookies and a $12 donation. Then each participant gives the $12 donation to the event organizer for the charity. Finally, each participant walks around the tables and collects a dozen cookies from the other participants' plates. Each attendee gets to consume and keep the dozen cookies that they collect. I once participated in a cookie exchange where attendees were also permitted to bring store-purchased cookies. This made it easier for busy people and those without an interest in cooking to attend.

This event can be held at an organization's office or a supporter's home. This works great as a third-party fundraiser, where the host uses the cookie exchange as a holiday party. The amount of donations raised by the fundraiser is directly in relation to the number of attendees, so the more participants the better. As a result, bigger spaces and larger invitee lists are preferred.

341. SPECIALTY PET SUPPLIES

People love their pets. For organizations that provide shelter and care for animals, a great fundraiser is selling specialty pet supplies. These may include items like custom collars, clothes, and booties. These can easily be made and donated by crafters. They can also be purchased via wholesalers. Some wholesalers include Lovelonglong (www.lovelonglong.com), Above and Beyond Style (www.pettease.com), Doggie Designer (www.doggiedesigner.com/whole

sale/wholesale.htm), Doggie Design (www.doggiedesign.com), and Fuzzy Butts (www.thefuzzybutts.com).

Sales of these goods can be done via e-newsletters, in the organization's office, via the web store, through retailers, and at tabling events. The highest sales success rate will likely come from sales at the shelter and in the web store.

342. PRIVATE COMMISSION

Recently, arts organizations have had to diversify their funding resources as traditional corporate underwriting support has dwindled. One great way to increase revenue from private donors is to invite community members to commission works. For example, an individual could pay a playwright $5000 to create a work as an anniversary present to their partner. Another example would be a private individual donating $3000 to commission an art exhibition from an art collective. In this way, the art is available to the community to enjoy and is especially dedicated to the individuals who fund it.

To cultivate this type of private commission, the organization's development staff should let past supporters and members know about this unique opportunity. By creating a sense of scarcity and stating that only a specific number of commissions per year are allowed, donors may speak up more quickly.

343. SPORTS LESSONS

Sports lessons are a great way for teams to raise money. The lessons can take the form of day camps for children or individual coaching for adults. It is common for high school sports teams to attend day camps at the local colleges. There, the teams would teach fundamentals of the sport to the high school students. Each morning, students are picked up and dropped off by their guardians. Lunches are packed. Camps cost about $100 per day and up, and are paid for either by the team or by the team members' parents. One camp I attended was three days long. It cost about $500. We spent the three days having college students give us advice and competing against other teams. There were about 700 attendees. The space was provided by the school. As a result, the organization made their annual operation budget from the three days of camp. One-on-one lessons cost more per hour and are the financial responsibility of the individual receiving the coaching.

344. JOURNALS

Journals are an easy and fun fundraiser for children. They are especially appropriate fundraisers for youth organizations that encourage writing, such as poetry clubs. The members of the club get together and decorate journals. Then they sell them at tabling events and through personal contacts. Journals can be either purchased inexpensively in bulk or created by taking paper, putting card stock on the front and back, and then stapling it together. Use blank paper for art journals or lined paper for writing journals. These journals typically cost less than $1 to produce, but can be sold for $5 depending on how creative the cover art or decorations are.

345. SPEED DATING

Speed dating is a fundraiser for singles clubs or adult associations. Attendees pay a fee and meet with several other participants for a maximum of 3 minutes each. At the end of each session, the organizer rings a bell and one of the participants gets up and moves to the next table. At the end of the event, each participant writes three people on their list in the order in which they would like to have a longer date with them. The organizer matches up people who are on each other's lists. Then, mingling and future date setting happens informally. Rates vary, but generally admission to these events is at least $20 per person. If space for the event is donated, then the event incurs no expenses besides the organizers' time. The more participants, the more fundraising income, so fill every seat.

346. SALVAGE SALE

A salvage sale is a fundraiser where members collect items they no longer use, clean them up, and bring them together for a sale. The sale typically lasts two days. Participants' goods are donated to the sale. Volunteers organize and manage the sale. Proceeds from the donated goods go directly to the cause. Income increases as donated goods and customers increase. When the sale is over, have any remaining goods collected by a thrift store or other charity shop. To maximize customer attendance, hold the sale at the same time each year in the spring or summer, depending on the temperature in the region.

347. Private Chef

One of the most interesting fundraisers I ever attended was a dinner where a private chef made food for about 10 attendees. The chef donated her time to the cause. Each attendee paid for the dinner. A volunteer hosted the event. We each learned about and tasted new and delicious dishes. The hosts prepared topics to keep the conversation as interesting as the cuisine. Attendees paid $30. The hostess donated the ingredients and beverages. The organization made $300 on this third party fundraiser. More valuable was that individual attendees then went on to organize private chef demonstration events for their friends and the donations grew exponentially. As the donations grew, so did the number of supporters in the community.

348. Personalized Address Book

Despite the popularity of online contact management systems, individuals still like the security that a hardcopy of their contacts provides. For this reason a personalized address book can be a successful fundraiser for organizations whose supporters are adults ages 30 and above.

Individuals preorder the address books. They have the owner's name on the cover and contact information on the inside cover, for if the book is ever lost. Some organizers are able to import data from the order's online contacts via an Excel spreadsheet. In each alphabetical section, additional spaces are made available for future contacts.

These address books should be preordered and prepaid. Get printing and binding quotes before determining the price of the address books. If possible, recipients should pick them up in person at the organization's office to save on shipping and administrative time. The more personalized the address book, the more that can be charged for them. If photos can be added, they become a precious keepsake.

349. SANDWICH COOKIES DIPPED IN CHOCOLATE

Few things are more delectable then sandwich cookies dipped in chocolate. This fundraiser is appropriate for nearly all nonprofit organizations, with the exclusion of groups focused on healthy eating. These cookies are an easy gourmet item that can be sold at special events, in tins via the web store, via tabling events, through volunteer fundraising sales, and door-to-door. I have seen individual sandwich cookies dipped in dark chocolate sell for $2 per cookie. This puts the profit per cookie at about $1.60.

350. BABYSITTING

A babysitting fundraiser is when members of a parents group watch each other's kids, and instead of accepting payment for themselves, they ask for donations to be given directly to a cause that all of the members support. In my experience, the ideal organization for this type of fundraiser is a children's charity. Typical babysitting rates vary greatly by region, number of children, and level of experience of the caregiver. Generally, $15 per hour, per child is appropriate for the fundraiser. No matter the cause, participants should only have individuals watch their children who they completely trust and who have past experience. Children are irreplaceable, so always error the side of caution when it comes to their well-being. This includes only using caregivers with references, background checks, and up-to-date CPR certifications. Liability insurance is a must.

351. CELEBRITY SWEEPSTAKES

Organizations lucky enough to get the support of professional athletes or other celebrities can raffle off the opportunity to meet the celebrity. I recently participated in a fundraiser where individuals donated $5 per chance to meet the celebrity. The more that a donor gave, the more chances they had to win. Check with the local municipality to determine if a raffle or gambling licenses is required for such a fundraiser. In this way, a celebrity can use their personal pull to increase publicity, support, and funds for an organization. Keep the cost per chance low to maximize income. Use a random number generator like www.Random.org to find a winner. Make sure security is provided for the celebrity at the event.

352. Meet the Pro

For organizations with access to a professional instructor or coach, a meet-the-pro event can raise significant funds. Individuals buy tickets to attend an event. At the event, they have the opportunity to meet with the professional instructor. The more high-level the professional and the event, the more the organization can charge for tickets and the more individuals will attend. This is a great fundraiser for sports teams, athletic clubs, or alumni associations.

353. Art Rental

Art rental is a way for art organizations to raise funds by utilizing their resources. Oversized works of art are a great way for realtors to cover walls in sample units and increase sales. The organization stores the donated pieces when they are not being used. Over time, the organization will make more money in rental fees then it would make just by selling the art. To arrange to rent out the organization's works, contact commercial realtors and developers in the community. You may be surprised at how eager they are to support a cause while decorating their sample units.

354. Bartending Class

Bartending classes are fun social events for organizations with a social mission. A bartender donates their talents, and a bar can donate the alcohol and space. The organization sells tickets for attendance as the source of fundraising income. This fundraiser works best for nonprofit organizations for adults ages 21 to 40. Whenever an event has alcohol, there is an opportunity for added liability issues. Please speak with the organization's insurer before planning this event.

355. PAINTING

Painting is a service fundraiser where members paint walls, fences, and furniture. They donate their time. Customers pay a premium, and the funds go to the organization. Customers also pay for the paint, brushes and tarps. The more individuals who are performing the service of painting, and the more customers, the greater the fundraising results. Painting fundraisers need adult volunteers to do the painting, so this fundraiser is not appropriate for youth groups.

356. DECK OF PERSONALIZED PLAYING CARDS

Selling decks of personalized playing cards is a unique fundraiser for organizations with volunteers to do the fundraising. The unit cost for the cards and the sale prices are very low. As a result, the income per unit sold is low. So, for significant funds to be raised, a high volume of playing decks must be sold. Card customizing companies include Ad Magic Promotional Advertising (www.admagic.com), Your Playing Cards (www.yourplayingcards.com), Monogrammatiks (www.mo nogrammatiks.com), and Palaimon Cards (www.palaimoncards.com). Compare quotes to maximize profit.

357. MINGLE AND MEET THE EXPERTS

Mingle and Meet the Experts is a networking event where a group of experts on one topic attend, are introduced, and give advice on a specific topic. Other attendees pay an entrance fee which serves as the fundraising income. When I organized Mingle and Meet the Experts events, I utilized donated space and asked for a suggested donation from attendees. I planned topics for the event that were of interest to members to increase attendance. This fundraiser is ideal for professional and business associations.

358. Private Performance

For musical and performance arts organizations, a private performance can be a way to raise funds and build a relationship with a donor. Private performances can be arranged at the auditorium where performances are normally held, or at a location of the donor's choice for a cost premium. The larger the number of performers, the greater the donation needed to secure a private performance. In some cases, arts organizations can expand their income by selling half-price admissions to their rehearsals. This can be done in addition to smaller group private performances.

359. Fondue Fling

A Fondue Fling is a fundraiser where attendees pay for a specific amount of fruit and cookies. They then get to dip these in melted chocolate using fondue sticks. The location and ingredients should be donated. Participants should pay a premium for the fondue. Additionally, organizers can sell coffee and/or champagne to increase revenue. This is a great third-party fundraiser for individuals who want to raise funds in their own home for a cause that is dear to them.

360. Emergency Kits

Emergency kits are a good fundraiser because they are useful items that can be inexpensively constructed and sold for a premium. For ideas about first aid kit contents, research the kits that are available at local stores. The more expensive the items in the kits, the more the organization will need to charge for them. Kits can also be specialized from basic home first aid kits to car kits. They should be sold via volunteer fundraisers' networks of friends and family and via the organization's web store.

361. Bubble Play

Bubble plays are a great fundraiser for parents groups with young children. Organizers use bubble machines to make tons of bubbles for children to play in. Each child that attends gets their own container of bubbles, too. Income is raise through fees paid by parents to attend the bubble play with their child. Charges can be increased if children are provided with snacks and juice at the bubble play.

362. Field Day

Field days are fun events in which children and/or adults participate in various outdoor games. This is a great fundraiser for school and youth groups to organize. The more different types of activities being held, the more likely individuals are to want to attend. Each activity should be supervised and organized by volunteers. The cost of admission to the field day provides income to the nonprofit organization. Field day events can include croquet, badminton, obstacle courses, sack races, and other fun outdoor games.

363. Automobile Wraps

Automobile wraps are advertisement wraps that cover the majority of the vehicle where there aren't windows, mirrors, or lights. Automobile wraps are a great way to promote your organization and spur online donations. Include basic organization information including the logo, name, purpose, and website on the wrap. Apply wraps to all organization cars. Super supporters may see the wraps and want to buy them for their vehicles, as well. The more wrapped vehicles in the community, the more awareness is created by the campaign.

Many companies make and apply removable wraps for automobiles. Check with local vendors to find deals. Organizations might be able to get wraps for the organization itself donated with the provision that the donating company is listed on the wrap as an organization sponsor. Supporters who come forward wanting wraps will purchase the wraps from the marketing company that donated them to the organization.

Many organizations can benefit from vehicle wraps. The exceptions to this are environmental or conservation organizations. They should not affiliate themselves with all types of vehicles, and may have to be more discerning in their wrap placement.

364. Mindful Massage

A mindful massage event is a fundraiser where one or more trained massage therapists donate their services. Event attendees donate $2 per minute to the organization or $30 per 15 minutes of a treatment. Participants can submit payment in the form of cash or checks made out to the organization. This event allows a massage therapist to develop their business by offering a free sample of their service. It also raises money for a good cause.

A mindful massage event can be offered anywhere from a kiosk at a shopping center to an office complex to even a religious center. The key to success is a good location with great signage and walking traffic in the area. Make sure that the signs clearly state what organization will receive the funds, and the minimum donation rate. If the traffic in the area is too frequent to be relaxing, then consider playing white noise such as ocean waves. It is helpful for more than one professional to be offering the service at a time in order to maximize income. Additionally, it is helpful for a volunteer to be present to help sell services, collect money, and give out further information about the cause.

365. Donate

Why don't you donate? Employees, supporters, founders, and volunteers are great sources of donations. If everyone gives a little, a lot can be accomplished. Be a good steward of the funding and goods the organization receives, and be respectful of volunteers' time and talents. The rest will fall into place. Happy Fundraising!

CPSIA information can be obtained at www.ICGtesting.com
Printed in the USA
242002LV00004B/9/P